ZBIGNIEW KUPCZYNSKI

ART WARRIOR

© 2003 Zbigniew Kupczynski

All rights reserved. No part of this book may be reproduced in any form or by any means without the written permission of the publisher except by a reviewer who may quote passages in a review.

National Library of Canada Cataloguing in Publication

Kupczynski, Zbigniew, 1928-
Art warrior / Zbigniew Kupczynski.

ISBN 1-894694-22-8

1. Kupczynski, Zbigniew, 1928- 2. Painters–Canada–Biography.
I. Title.

ND249.K85A2 2003   759.11   C2003-905179-X

Drawings: Zbigniew Kupczynski
Editing: Paul Vanderham • Jo Blackmore
Proofreading: Arlene Prunkl
Cover Design: Eva Kupczynski
Text Design: Shannon Harvey • Rebecca Davies

Granville Island Publishing
212-1656 Duranleau
Vancouver, BC V6H 3S4
Tel: (604) 688-0320
Toll Free: 1-877-688-0320
www.GranvilleIslandPublishing.com

Printed in Canada

I dedicate this book to my family
and those who really appreciate my art.

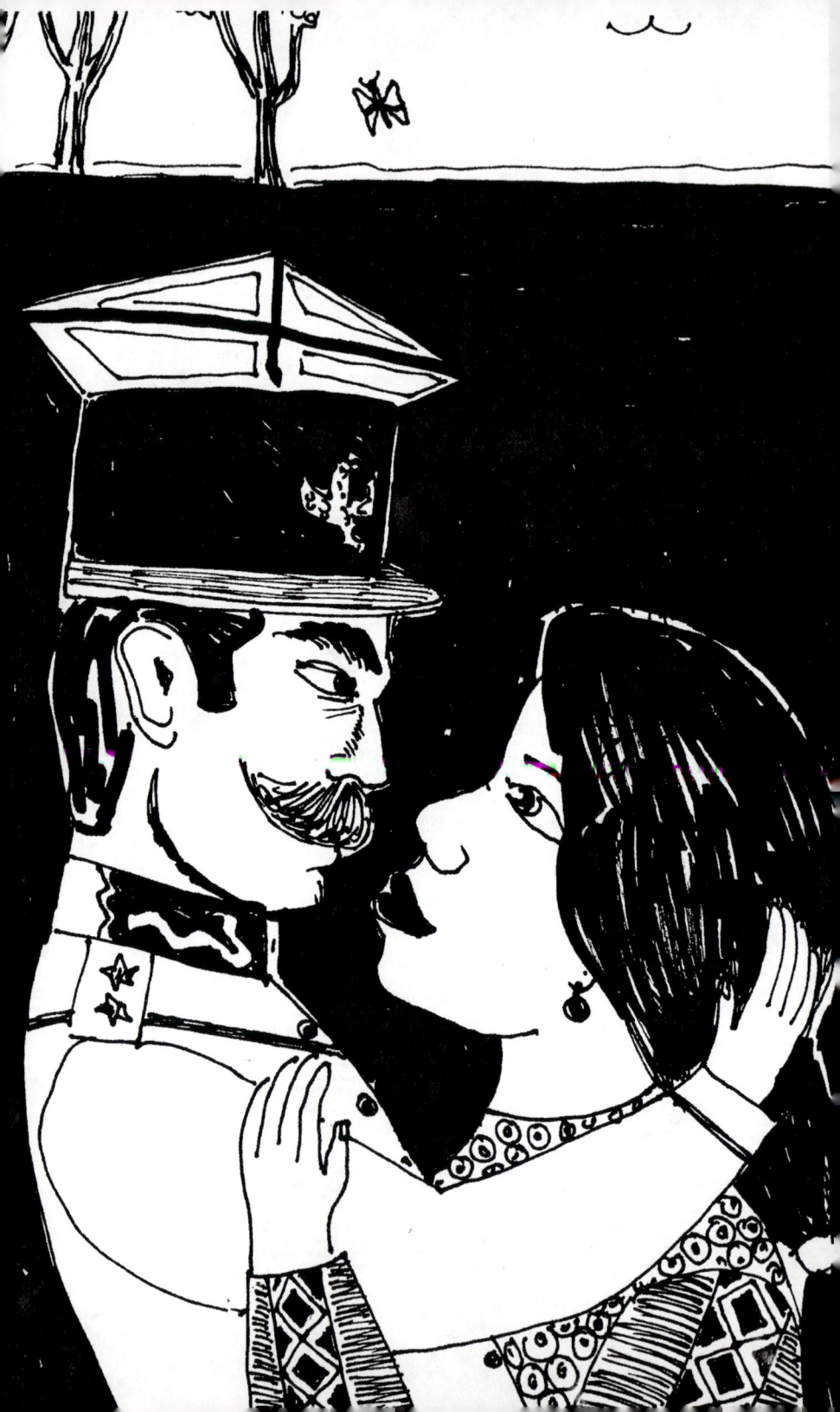

1

My father's grip on reality began to loosen during World War I while he lay in the trenches covered with mud and debris. The thunderous roar of the Prussian artillery fire rang in his ears, leaving him with a permanent tremor in his hands and a nervous twitch in his eye. Looking down at the lifeless bodies of his comrades, he murmured, "I have to get married." Then he crawled to the nearby forest. Soon after that the war ended.

Our hero received a commendation for his service on the front. He was made a lieutenant, given a new uniform, a shiny new sabre and a few medals. He shaved his beard, polished up his boots, and started going to the amusement park regularly. There, on the merry-go-round, he met Adela Zajac, my future mother. I was born some ten years later.

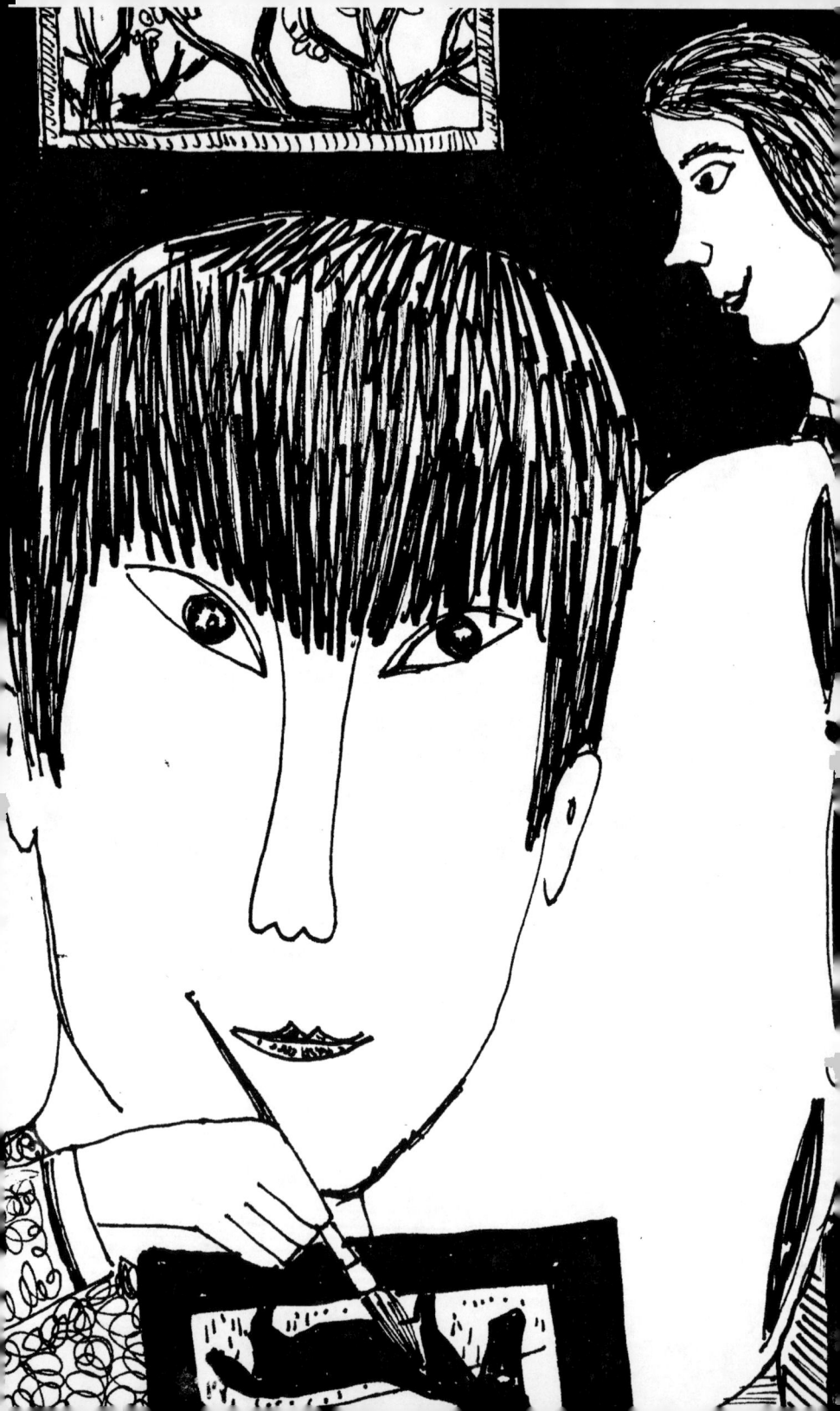

2

I remember my childhood in Kolomyja, a small town in the eastern territories of Poland, as if it were yesterday... the black cat Maciek, the neighbourhood dog Burek, and the two white rabbits. One day my father brought home a rooster. It was a very beautiful bird with green feathers and a red crest. It ate out of my hand and followed me around like a dog. All went along fine until I got sick with typhoid. I had a high fever and headaches. My parents took me to the hospital, where I stayed for three weeks. The medicine was not working. My grandmother Andula sent for some holy water, but that didn't help either.

One day Sister Agata brought me some crayons. "You have to do something with yourself," she said. "Why don't you start drawing colourful pictures?"

I took her advice. I drew a two-headed dragon, a king with a green face, and soldiers in steel armour tearing through a field on blue horses. I drew at least twenty pictures. My headaches stopped.

The doctor came to my room and said that there had been a miracle. "This was a very nasty case of typhoid," he

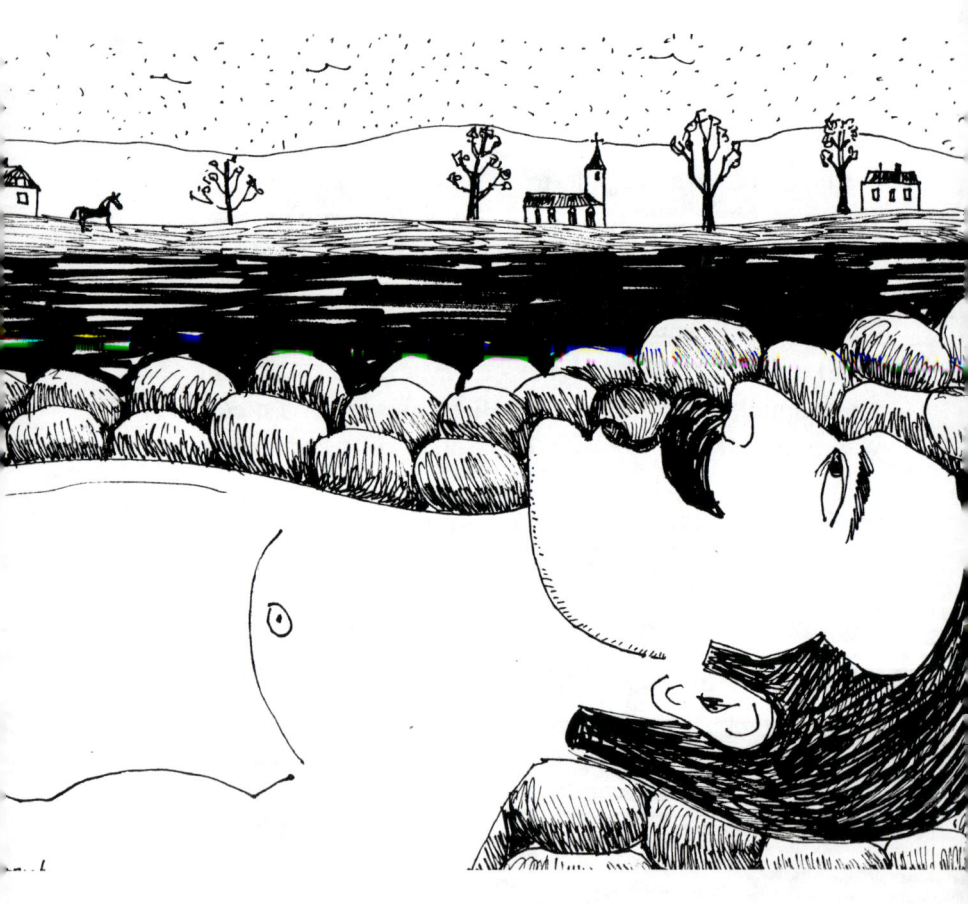

said to the nurse. "I wasn't sure if our patient would make it through the week."

On Sunday the nurse told me to get dressed. I was so weak that I fainted when I got out of bed. My father carried me to the waiting horse and carriage. We were soon making our way home. It was May. I looked at the smiling trees. The rhythmic sound of the horseshoes clattered against the pavement.

At home everything seemed the same as always. The vase with artificial flowers sat on the dining-room table, and father's sabre hung on the kitchen wall. The drawer where he kept his gun was locked, as always. The only thing missing was my rooster.

"What happened to my bird?" I asked my mother.

"I didn't tell you this because I didn't want to upset you, son," she said, "but your rooster got away while the gate was open and was hit by a car." I cried.

A week later, my next door neighbour Zdzisio Buleczke told me that my dear mother had lied to me. "I saw her sitting on the front steps of your house," he said. "She held the rooster between her legs and cut his throat."

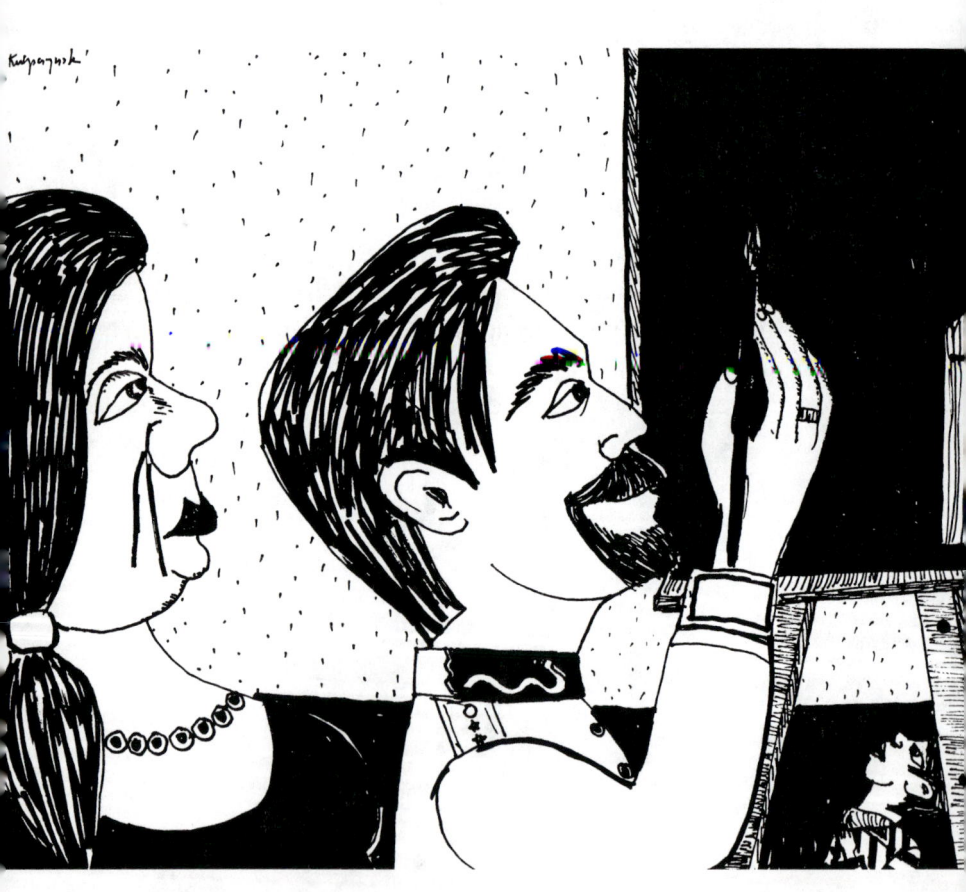

3

My father's pension amounted to 160 zloty a month ($40 Cdn). This was enough to cover the rent, food, clothing and other expenses. My father would buy strings for his violin, oil paints and tickets to the local cinema. Every week I watched Tarzan swinging from the trees, detectives dressed in plaid jackets and cowboys with their smoking guns. Often when I got home, I would try to imitate Tarzan. Standing in front of the mirror, I made wild sounds and pounded my bare chest.

As a retired lieutenant of the Polish Army, my father had a lot of free time on his hands. In the summer he would take me to play by the Prut River. The water was crystal clear and the fish shimmered under the surface. The bank was covered with white stones, which got quite hot under the sun and burned our bare feet. Back then I didn't know how to swim, so I frolicked in the shallow water while father lay resting on the white stones and staring at the blue sky above. Sometimes he whistled old army songs.

We would always come home content but hungry for the supper mother had waiting. We often devoured cumin soup and steaming young potatoes with buttermilk. After dinner father would nod off while reading his newspaper. I would sneak out on my tiptoes to the garden where I ate fresh berries straight off the shrubs. One day father announced that our apartment was too expensive and that we would have to move into something more affordable. Soon a big moving van appeared in front of our apartment building. The movers began to load our furniture. Two hours later the apartment was empty. My mother left last, carrying the cat in her arms.

We drove for twenty minutes, passing numerous streets, houses and shops. After driving by a school and a small chapel with a scruffy tower, we drove down a wide paved road. There were wheat fields on both sides, and you could hear the rustle of wheat swaying in the wind. In the distance I saw some red buildings and what looked like smoking factory stacks. We turned left, passed a small park, and stopped in the shade of a spruce tree growing in front of an old house.

"This is our new home," said father as he got out of the van.

The house had a large kitchen and three rooms. This was one room more than before, but the toilet was outside, connected to the house only by a narrow footpath. Mother was not pleased.

"This is how peasants live," she said.

"This is not a village!" father snapped. "It is only five kilometres from the city."

"Look at this," insisted my mother. "An officer of the Polish Army ends up living like a peasant."

"I am no longer an officer!" father protested. "I am a painter now."

"An artist, Dad, an artist," I said.

He liked my calling him an artist, but he didn't notice

that I winked at mother as I did so. I was only hoping that he would let me use his oil paints sometimes.

The next day I went for a walk to check out my new surroundings. Nestled amongst the trees, I found many more houses, actually a whole neighbourhood. I also discovered a grocery store, an Orthodox church and a Jewish cemetery. In the park, as I was passing under a tall tree, someone spat on my shirt. I looked up and met the icy blue eyes of a boy my age. I wiped my shirt and asked him why he was looking at me like that.

"You better get lost," he said, "we don't like strangers around here."

"It's easy to be a tough guy when you're hiding up in a tree," I responded.

"Not any more," he said as he slipped quickly down the trunk like a cat.

Next thing I knew he had punched me in the nose. I reciprocated with a fury that I didn't know I had in me, giving him a black eye. He kicked me in the knee. Before we tumbled into the ditch, I managed to bite his ear. Suddenly, we heard a clap of thunder and rain started pouring down. My opponent, whose name turned out to be Mundzio Rapinski, started to run towards the old brick factory. I followed his lead, racing him head to head. By the time we reached the factory, we were both soaking wet.

"I like guys who know how to fight," he said, taking out a pack of cigarettes. "Wanna smoke?"

I took a drag and, never having smoked before, immediately started to cough. While the rain pounded on the courtyard floor, Mundzio told me about his gang. "Come to the park tomorrow," he said. "I think you'll like it."

When I finally got home, soaking wet and covered with dirt, I had a bleeding nose. My father was not pleased.

"Take off your boots!" he shouted. "You're tracking mud in the house."

He was standing by his easel, working on a new masterpiece. Like most of his previous paintings, it featured a fall landscape and a romantic sunset of the kind he liked to fashion after the postcard images of an established Polish painter by the name of Rapacki. Father tirelessly copied every detail.

If anyone interrupted his work, he would get angry, muttering under his breath harsh epithets about people who don't have any appreciation for art. This drove mother crazy.

"Any idiot can copy!" she would yell. "Why don't you get yourself a job? It's impossible to make ends meet on your pension."

Father would then call her a birdbrain. Mother would turn red in the face and threaten to hang herself. I used to run away from their fights to the old brick factory.

One day, as I was standing at a nearby pond, someone pushed me in. I nearly drowned but by some miracle made it to shore. My brush with death really scared my parents and was one of the main reasons we soon moved back to the city.

Our new residence was a one-storey apartment block on Moniuszki Street. During the winter, when icicles shimmered through the windows, father played his violin. He stood with his legs spread wide, his back against the hot wood-burning stove. Sometimes he was so engrossed in his task that he could not smell the smoldering fabric of his jacket. His concerts would take place in the evening while I lay in my bed, covering my ears with the pillow, trying to escape the harrowing sounds. My mother hid in the church.

I was in fifth grade when World War II broke out. I

remember father coming through the door dressed in his old army officer's uniform. He took his sabre off the wall, buckled his revolver to his waist, and said he was going out to defend his country. He kissed me on the cheek and, without even looking at my mother, he left the house, never to return. Mother put on a new dress, applied some red lipstick, and went to church. As I looked out the window after she had gone, I could hear the sound of artillery fire in the distance. By nightfall the Russian troops had moved into Kolomyja. I began painting soldiers.

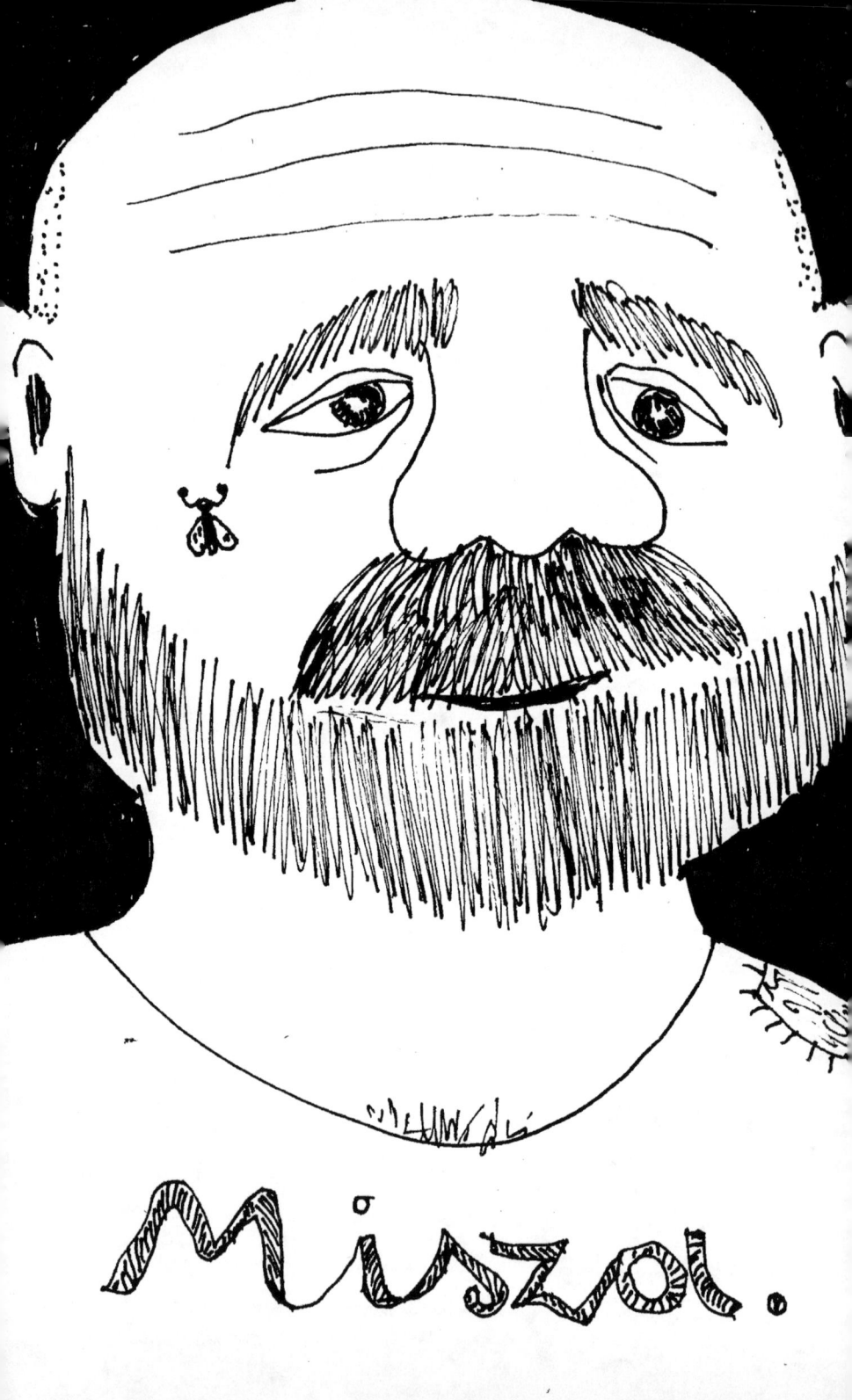

4

His name was Misza Baran. A short, big-boned man with a round face, he had a red nose and beady eyes. Everyone called him Miszka. He hung around the city streets panhandling or looking for work. Before the war he had spent some time in jail for his left-wing convictions. A lazy bum who expected life to be handed to him on a silver platter, he hated people with aspirations. My grandfather, Maks, gave him a job on the farm, but he sat around doing nothing. Then he took to stealing chickens. One day Grandfather caught him red-handed. He grabbed him by the lapels, lifted him up, threw him against a haystack, and said, "If you ever show your face here again, I'll break your legs!"

When the Russian troops took over Kolomyja, Miszka decided to get even. He put a red ribbon on his arm and pretended he was a die-hard Communist. He told the authorities that Maks Zajac was a dangerous reactionary and a threat to the working class. Two Russians with assault rifles took my grandfather away in handcuffs. The next day there was a hearing at City Hall. The hearing committee consisted of five Russian officers and one Pole, an ex-prosecutor by the name of Alex Fajdak. He was a rat-faced little man who collaborated with the Russians.

After Miszka finished presenting his list of lies about grandfather, Alex Fajdak said he believed that Maks Zajac was a disgrace to the working class who should be sent to a work camp in Siberia. Miszka was pleased. Grandfather turned as pale as a sheet. Then a miracle happened, something that none of us could have predicted: a Russian general with grey hair and a bushy moustache walked energetically across the room. With blue eyes that looked straight ahead from behind the gold frames of his glasses, he quickly surveyed the accusers, then glanced at Grandfather. A look of surprise appeared on his face. "Maks?" he said. "Maks Zajac?"

The general was Igor Kowalow, the right hand man to Marshal Zukow, who was in charge of Polish affairs in the eastern territories. It turned out that he and grandfather had grown up together in the part of Poland that, in the days of their youth, was under Czarist occupation. As young men they attended the same school and often competed for the affection of pretty girls.

As soon as General Kowalow came on the scene, the whole affair went smoothly. After reading the documents accusing Grandfather, he tore them up and threw them in the garbage, saying, "the Russian Army has more important things to do!" Miszka mumbled something under his breath, but to no avail. General Igor's car, a black chauffeur-driven sedan, was parked in front of City Hall. After the two friends had climbed in, the general decided that he had worked up a thirst dealing with all that nonsense and invited Grandfather to a nearby pub, where they drank beer and talked about old times.

"You haven't changed a bit," observed the general.

"You neither," said Grandfather.

"Oh, no. I've changed. I've definitely changed," said

the general.

Then they ordered another round. After a couple of hours things warmed up. Grandfather and the general started to sing old racy songs.

"You have to leave here, Maks," the general said eventually. "Things around here will get ugly very soon. The KGB plans to move one of their divisions into City Hall. That son-of-a-bitch Karasyn will be stationed here." He looked kindly at Maks. "We have a refugee agreement with the Germans . . . but you must have family on the other side."

"My son lives in Warsaw," said Maks.

"Good. You won't have any problems then."

"What about my family?" asked Grandfather.

"You'll take them with you. I'll arrange for it."

They agreed that Grandfather would report the following morning to pick up the documents. He took his leave of Igor and walked home slowly on trembling legs. After stopping to relieve himself near a lamppost, he zipped up his pants and said to himself, "Maks, it's time to pack up and get the hell out of here."

Thanks to the Russian general, we had no trouble getting on the train to Przemysl, situated on the Russian-German border. There were seven of us: Grandpa Maks, Grandma Andula, Aunt Lusia, Uncle Michal, seven-year-old cousin Wanda, my mother, Adela and me. Since the train stopped at every station, the trip took nine hours. At Przemysl the Germans inspected our papers and belongings very carefully before allowing us to pass through the refugee camp. They disinfected everything we owned, including our clothes. By the time we boarded the express train to Warsaw several hours later, we were tired, hungry and stinking of disinfectant. I fell asleep immediately and dreamed of the brick factory in our former town.

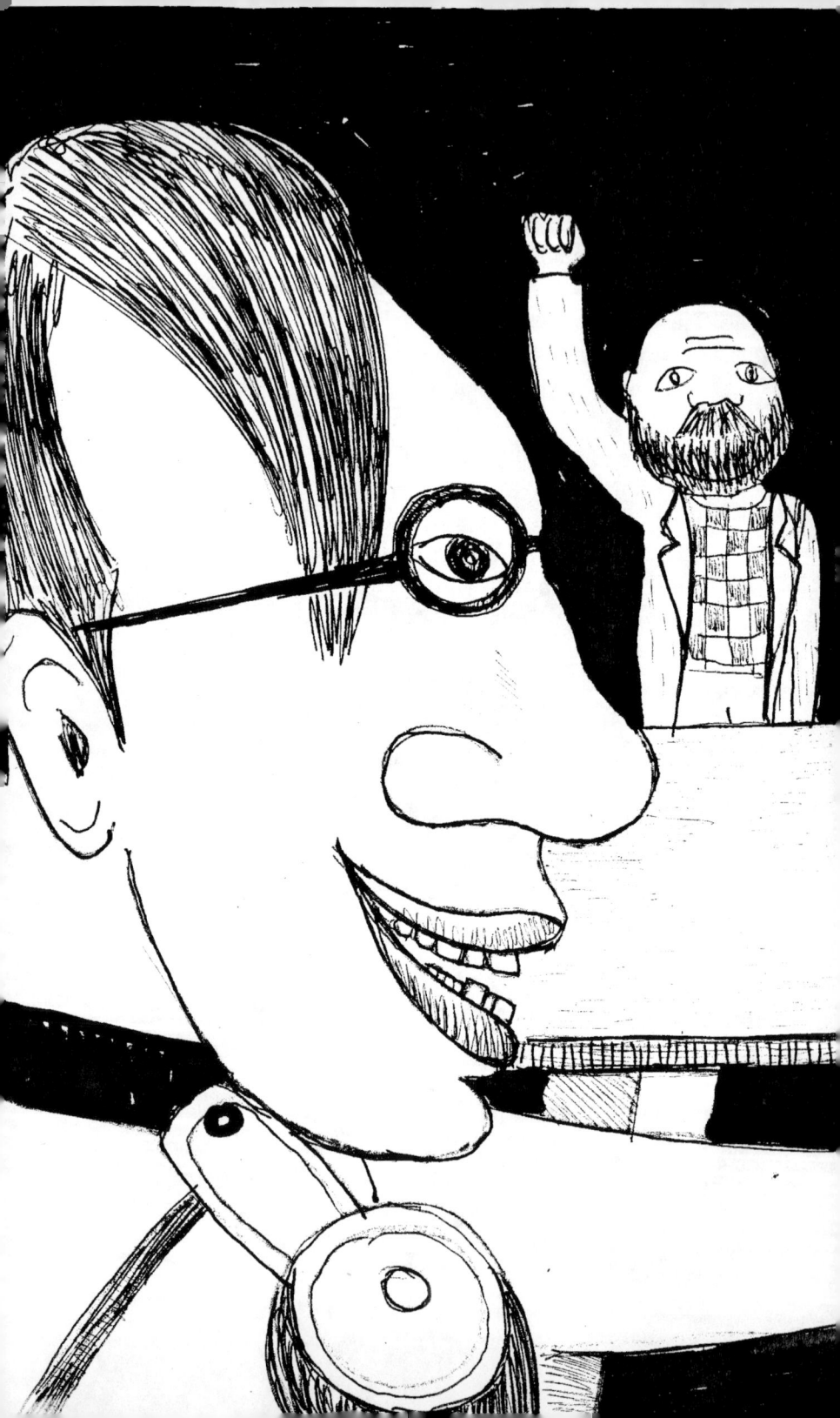

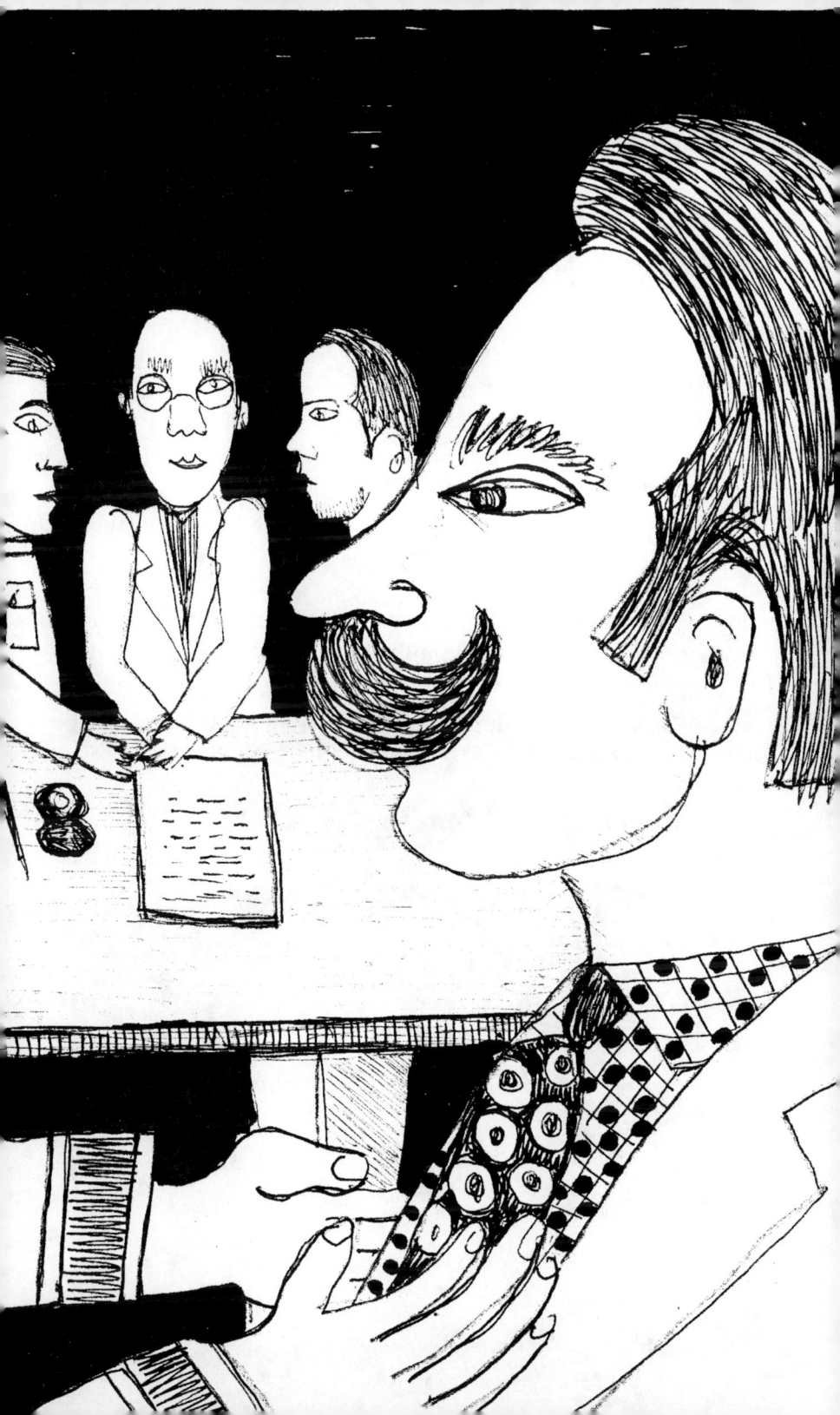

I was with a bunch of naked teenagers jumping from the second storey of a building into the thick chocolate-coloured water of a clay pit. We rolled around in the mud and then ran out into the clover field uttering battle cries. That's when we made a strange discovery. A man in a black hat was lying on top of a naked, red-haired woman. Her arms were wrapped around him. He had a badly blemished back. His pants were down at his ankles and his fat rump looked like a big, white ship rocking on the ocean. Mundzio threw mud at them. A few other boys picked up some nettles. The couple scrambled to their feet and, after the man managed to pull up his pants, they disappeared into the wheat field. "We scared the daylights out of them," said Mundzio. "That will be the last time they play doctor."

The wheels of the train made a rhythmic sound. I could hear the train whistle in my sleep. Still dreaming, I rolled over and the man in the black hat emerged from amongst the wheat. His face was somehow familiar to me—he had a red nose and beady eyes—but I couldn't remember how I

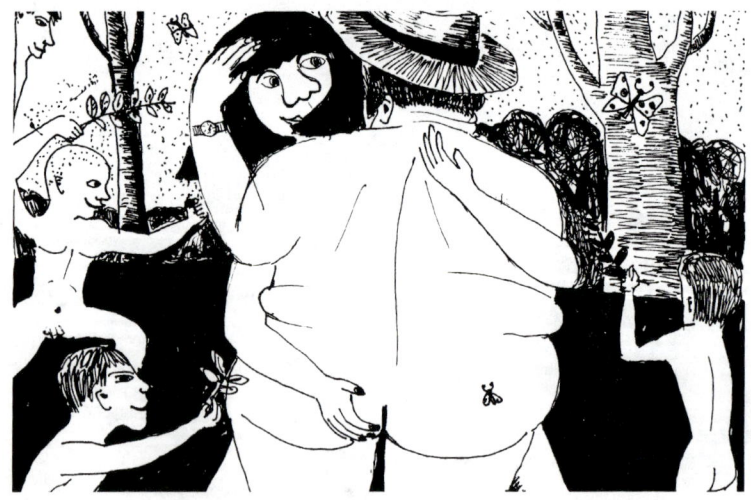

knew him. "I'll get you for this!" he shouted, waving his fists and running towards me. Suddenly I was all alone in the field: small, defenceless, dressed in a little sailor's outfit. Why was I wearing this outfit? I wore it only to church. He was only a few steps away. I tried to run, but I froze. He reached out as if to grab my hair. I felt his breath on my face . . . I gathered all my strength and . . . woke up.

I opened my eyes. I was drenched with sweat. The train was rushing uphill, leaving behind the green fields, spotted cows and white houses. My mother was knitting and talking to my grandmother in a low voice so as not to wake me up. Grandpa was reading a newspaper. At the other end of the compartment Uncle Michal was snoring and Aunt Lusia and Wanda were playing checkers.

I closed my eyes again and drifted. Somewhere in the distance I could hear the faint sound of a violin. I was sitting under a large tree looking out onto the horizon. Amongst yellow sunflowers I could see the outhouse. Miszka Baran was running towards it. He was holding a large, rusty key. He put it into the lock, turned it and disappeared inside. A familiar voice spoke to me from the tree above. It was Mundzio Rapinski. He slid down the tree and said, "I'm gonna lock the bastard in there." He ran up to the outhouse, put the padlock through the hasp and turned the key. For a while there was silence. Then the man inside seemed to suddenly awake. He started pounding at the door. The tiny structure shook so violently it appeared that it could fall apart at any minute.

"I'll kill you! I will kill you!" Miszka's voice rang in my ears. Then someone tapped me on the shoulder.

"Wake up son, we're almost there," said my mother.

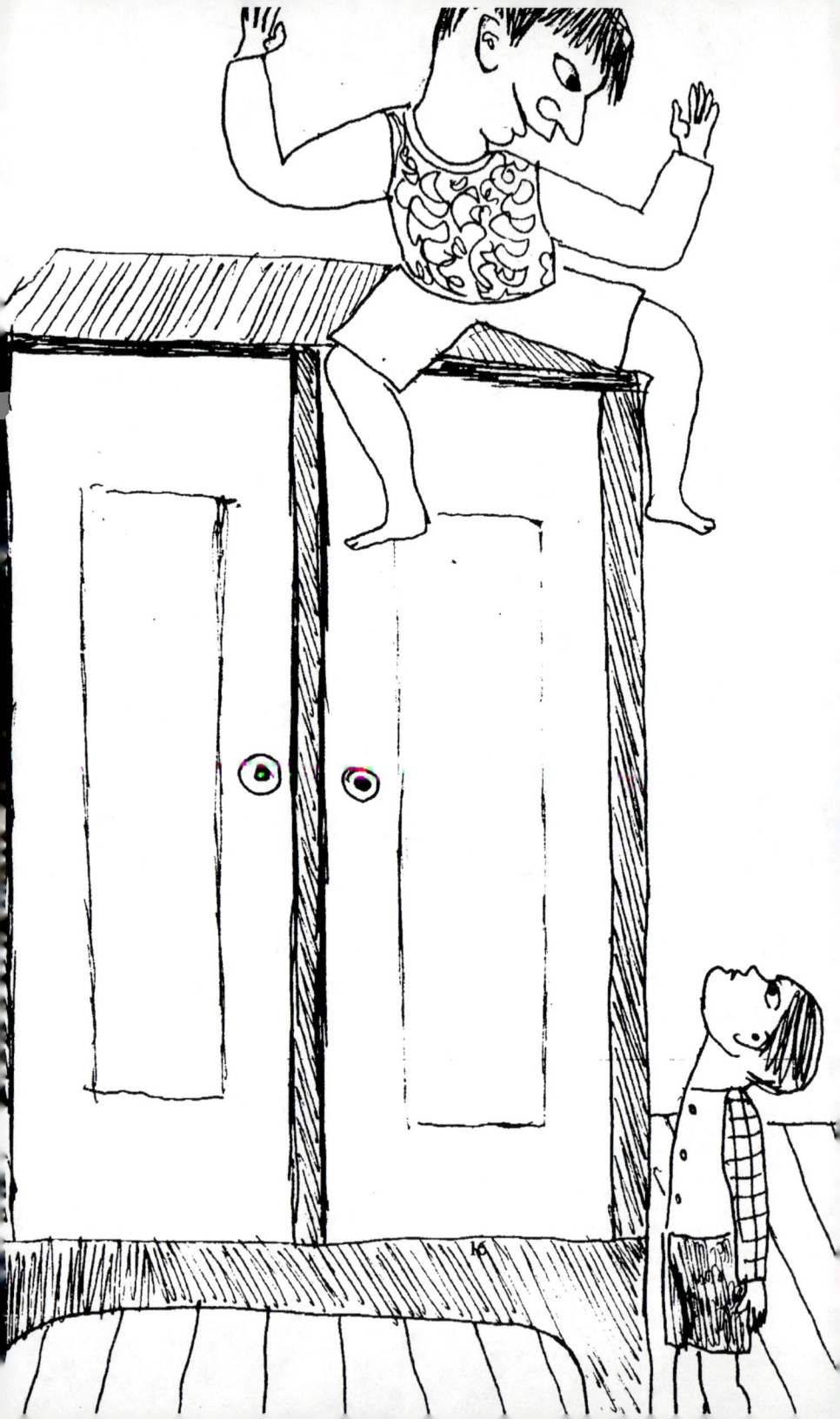

5

For a while we lived in Milanowek at my Uncle Marian's house. Everything would have been perfect, if not for Aunt Irka. A small, shriveled, bow-legged witch, she could not get used to seeing the seven new faces that took over the largest room in her house. Grandfather gave her food money, which he earned by occasionally selling a ring or a bracelet from the sizeable jewelry collection he had managed to smuggle across the border.

Uncle Marian was a sickly man. Although he had asthma, he continued to smoke, unable to shake the habit. To keep the peace in the family, he always agreed with his wife. As a result, the witch would always get her way. Their only son, Jurek, took a different approach: when he didn't want to do something he would climb on top of the dresser and yell the word *arse* in different languages, including Russian, German, Yiddish and Ukrainian. He even knew how to swear in the dialect of some East African tribe. I despised him. A few years older than I, he never missed a chance to bully me. He was especially fond of making me do things I didn't want to do, like arranging the books on the shelves or painting the wheels on his bike. One day he stole a silver coin from his mother's purse. When his father found out and disciplined him, he told everyone that I had put him up to it. Even Maks, who was not crazy about me, took my side.

"He is a piece of work, this one," he said. "But he is no thief."

On this one occasion, Uncle Marian sided with Grandfather, which drove Aunt Irka crazy.

"Instead of taking your son's side, you're siding with a bum!" she lamented.

A huge fight broke out. Everyone got involved. Finally, Aunt Irka told all of us to go to hell. Grandfather was so offended that he started to look for a new place for us to live. We soon moved into a one-room apartment in Warsaw, which had a window overlooking the vegetable garden. Crammed to near-suffocation into this small space, the seven of us tried to survive the German occupation. Uncle Michal got a job at the railway. My mother worked in a toy store and Aunt Lusia managed a furniture store.

Grandfather's health was failing. Poor diet and constant worry took their toll on him, turning a tall, athletic, larger-than-life man into a hypochondriac who complained constantly and took his temperature several times a day. He became jumpy and suspicious of everything, and he had a bone to pick with everyone: my mother for not raising me properly, Uncle Michal for snoring at night, and Grandma Andula for stuffing his pillow too hard.

The only person remaining in his favour was Wanda, Aunt Lusia's daughter. She was a year younger than me, had a round, chubby face and a nose that resembled a flattened potato. Aunt Lusia would force-feed her, pushing spoonfuls into her mouth while counting, "One, two, three . . ." as she waited for the child to swallow. If Wanda refused to eat any more, Aunt Lusia would slap her face. Then Wanda would eat some more while Aunt Lusia continued to count, "four, five, six . . ."

My school was just around the corner. I liked my art teacher. She gave us complete freedom as to our subject matter. I drew tanks, cannons and soldiers. I was apparently quite good because the teacher always used my work as an example for others to follow. My favourite subjects were Polish, history and art. My life back then was really not so bad, except that Grandfather always managed to find fault with me. My hands would be too dirty or my hair too long. And every time I picked up a crayon to draw he would get angry. One day I drew a caricature of him with a thermometer in his mouth. Everyone laughed, even Uncle Michal, who normally didn't have a sense of humour. As a result, my relationship with Grandfather deteriorated even further. One day at the supper table, he said, "Tomorrow we'll put him in a boarding school. I've had just about enough of this unmanageable brat!"

When Mother started to cry at these words, Aunt Lusia tried to calm her down.

"Zbyszek is a very active child," she said. "This apartment is getting too small for him. In boarding school, he will meet boys his age . . ."

Mother didn't want to let me go, but Grandfather's mind was made up. So one day not long after his pronouncement, I found myself in a drab old building on Senatorska Street, holding a small suitcase in my hand.

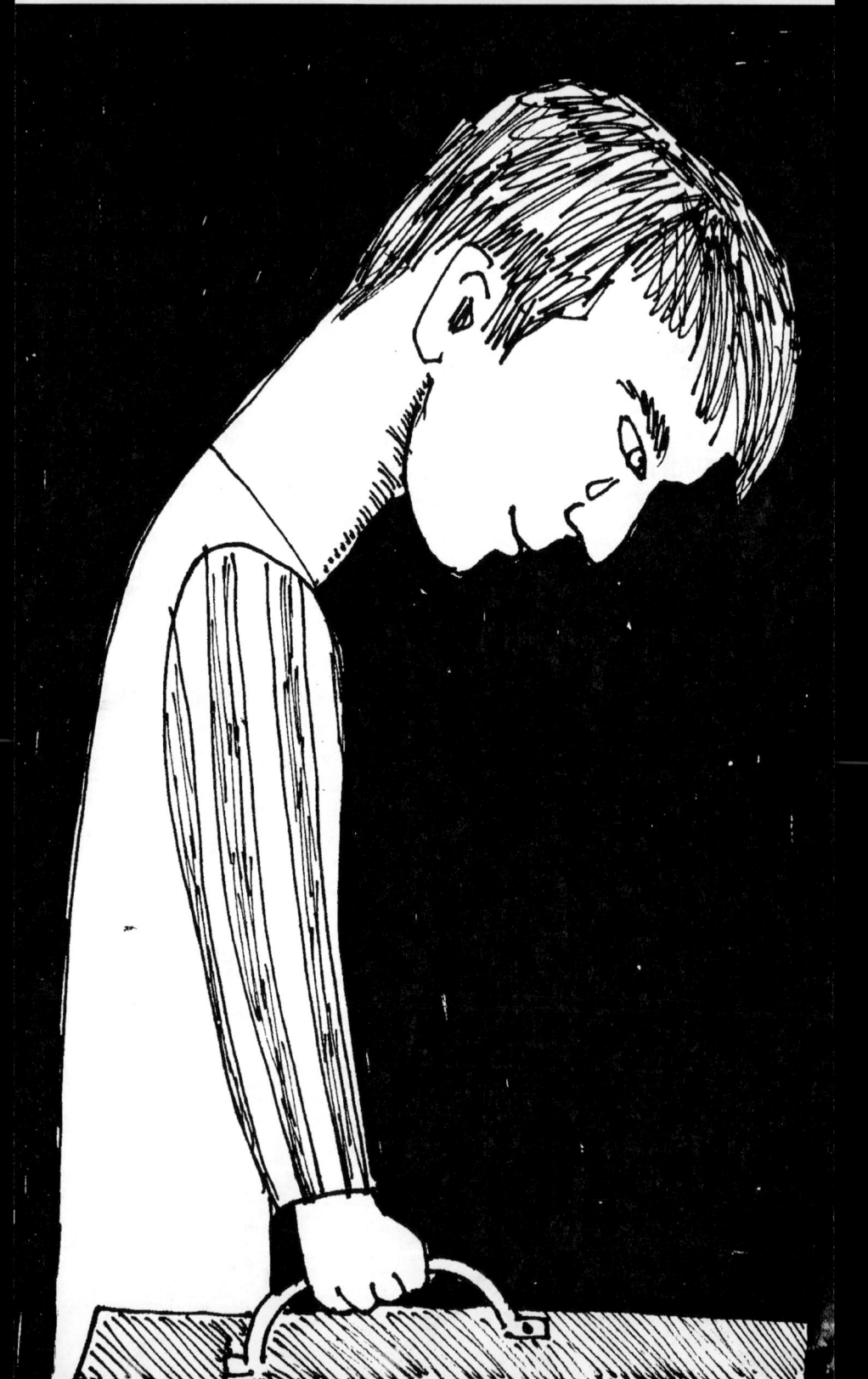

6

The dorm for my age group (nine to sixteen), located on the seventh floor, consisted of several bedrooms, a large dining hall and a white painted kitchen with a fat chef. Mr. Gniadosz was our teacher and also the principal. We called him "Horse." In his younger days he had intended to be a priest, but he fell in love with a violet-eyed blond and left the seminary for her. When she dumped him later, he almost committed suicide, but he finally came to his senses and became a teacher at Senatorska Street. He believed strongly in order, discipline and physical exercise. Every morning before breakfast, we had gym and a prayer session. "Healthy body, healthy soul," he would say.

For the most part, I got along with the boys in my dorm room quite well, with the exception of Kalita. He was of medium height with long arms that he put to constant use stealing. He had a reputation for being a troublemaker and a squealer. He was quite large for his thirteen years but always seemed to pick on boys smaller than himself. He disliked me from the start. He resented the fact that my clothes were always clean and pressed while he wore an old sweater with holes under his armpits.

"Let's see what you got in that suitcase," he said to me when I first walked through the door.

"A machine gun," I joked.

Two of the older boys started to laugh. Kalita, despite his size, was still too small to stand up to them, but he gave me the evil eye.

"We'll talk later," he said in a threatening voice.

Jurek Szablowski, whose bunk was beside the window, warned me: "You have to watch out for him. He is a vindictive scoundrel. He eavesdrops and then goes and tells Horse. Many of us have gotten into trouble because of him."

One day, with breakfast scheduled to start in fifteen minutes, I walked out onto the balcony. I liked to watch the street below and occasionally spit on the passersby. This time I aimed for a man on a bicycle. My aim was good. The spit landed right on his beret. He didn't even notice. "When he gets home," I thought as I watched the man disappear in the distance, "his wife or neighbour will tell him that someone has spit on his head." The metallic sound of the gong announced breakfast was ready. I tried to get back into the room, but someone had locked it from the inside. For a split second, I saw Kalita's smiling face.

"Open up!" I yelled, pounding on the door. I could hear Kalita laughing inside.

The window to the dining hall was open and only about nine feet away. I tried not to look down. Finally, my hand reached the windowsill. I held on tight, pulled myself up and jumped right onto the dining hall floor. Horse was not impressed.

"Are you expecting a medal for that?" he asked, pulling me by the ear. "If you're so talented, why don't you get yourself a job at the circus?" Then he threw me out the door, saying, "I'll deal with you after breakfast."

It turned out that he was not kidding. He soon came by my room, where I was sitting hungry and mad, gave me a letter for my grandfather, and sent me home. After the long walk (I had no money for the tram), I arrived famished and exhausted. My mother was sitting alone sewing. "Everyone has gone to the woods to pick wild mushrooms," she said, handing me a glass of milk. I drank hungrily.

The letter from Horse described the whole incident. The school made it clear that, in their view, I was a very irresponsible individual who took unnecessary risks with my life, and they did not want to be held accountable, if, God forbid, something unfortunate should happen to me. Consequently, it would be best for everyone involved if I attended school elsewhere. Grandfather was not pleased. He warned me to watch myself. "You can live with us, but remember that if you ever make me angry, even in the slightest, your own mother will not be able to help you—and you'll have only yourself to blame."

I promised to behave myself and kept my word. I went to school in the morning, did my homework in the afternoon, then played with Jurek and Grzesiek, the vegetable grower's sons, who were both my own age. Sometimes they helped their father selling tomatoes. When their father was not there, a good portion of the money from sales tended to find its way into the boys' pockets. They always had cigarettes, chocolate and comic books from the corner store. The comic books were especially important, since they provided us with our heroes: Bob Hunter, Ghost Rider of the Wild West; Ken Maynard, Gunslinger; and Leonardo Pratto, Ace Detective. We lived then in a dream world of our own making, one that shut out the grim reality all around us: the incessant persecution of the Poles by the Nazis, the continuous street round-ups and the constant threat of being sent to concentration camps. One day, on my way home, through the window of a tram, I saw a man in a raincoat with a gun being pursued by several Nazis with dogs. He disappeared around a corner. I don't know what happened next. The tram turned from Marszalkowska to Pulawska Street. The man with the gun was probably a member of the underground army.

One day, a friend of mine took me to an apartment building on Madalinski Street. That was where the secret cinema of Mr. Edzio was located. In the small, smoky room a bald man in glasses was conducting a secret screening of a silent movie starring Charlie Chaplin. Charlie, a funny man with a cane, was being chased by a fat policeman. They chased each other around a street lamp. Charlie kicked the policeman in the butt, knocking him into a ditch. Charlie took off his bowler hat and bowed to the law. The policeman got up from the ditch and stroked his moustache with the back of his hand. Then to our great delight the chase began again, and so it went until the projector jammed and the screen went dark.

As Mr. Edzio made repairs, he said, "Patience, my boys, everything will be fine in a moment. Stay calm." Naturally, this was our cue to horse around. Soon one boy had the contents of his jacket pocket cut out with a razor and another ended up with shoe polish on the back of his shirt. As long as we didn't try to destroy the screen or the chairs, Mr. Edzio let us have our fun.

In the summer I would go to the beach beside the Poniatowski Bridge. Part of the beach was set aside for sports. The facilities there included weights, a gym horse and a basketball court. The springboard was nine feet high. I learned to do various flips: forward, backward, feet first, head first, you name it. The sports area was the meeting place for many successful Polish athletes, including Gierutto, the former pentathlon champion, and Antoni Raska, the former boxing champion. They would practice there in their free time to stay in shape, and they would encourage teenagers like myself to train. Raska convinced me to start boxing more seriously at the club on Hoza Street, where I ended up training for two whole years. During that time I fought at least thirty fights, winning twenty-six. My left hook was dynamite. I danced in the ring like a ballerina. My coach Grzesiuk predicted a career for me in boxing. Unfortunately, this praise went to my head; I started taking my opponents lightly.

One day a short, stout man showed up in the ring. His face like a block of wood, his neck thick as a tree trunk, and his shoulders as wide as a house, he looked at me as if he wanted to eat me alive. My first punch landed on his face with great precision. He responded with two short swings, one a left and one a right. I caught both easily on my gloves. Blockhead then leapt forward, wanting to fight from a medium reach. I caught him with a strong left hook, which would have knocked any normal opponent flat on the boards. Blockhead, however, only turned crimson, thirsting for my blood. He began to swing furiously, his punches whizzing through thin air this way and that. I danced confidently in the midst of this flurry, landing punches of my own squarely on my opponent's nose, which soon began to look like a rotten tomato. Thinking I had the fight won, I chased Blockhead around the ring, tormenting him with hard punches, pounding on his face as if it was a drum on which I could beat out any rhythm I liked. Then, as I was winding up to deliver yet another blow, I carelessly neglected to cover my face. Seizing his chance,

Blockhead hit me with a ferocious right that made the ceiling collapse on my head. Before I knew it, I was lying stunned on the boards. Someone sprayed water in my face. I opened my eyes and met the glare of my trainer. He was not impressed with my defeat. Later, in the dressing room, my opponent's whistling goaded me to say, "You won because I opened myself up unnecessarily. I would bet that on a point count I would always win." Blockhead responded by chuckling mischievously and saying, "If you ever beat me, I'll give you a hundred zloty bill."

Unfortunately, there was never occasion for a rematch. My opponent, for unknown reasons, stopped coming to the club and soon the Warsaw Uprising broke out, putting an end to our games. At first, I remember, the Uprising itself seemed like a game of sorts. The group of rebels who gathered in the Królikarnia, the open field behind our street, seemed dressed for some sort of carnival. Some wore coonskin caps, others colourful bandanas. Together, they emerged armed with rifles, pistols, and hand-grenades, each wearing a red and white band on his sleeve bearing the inscription "A.K." (for Armia Krajowa, the Polish Underground Army). I watched them disperse into the streets of the Mokotow District of Warsaw, envying them their exciting adventure.

For several hours peace prevailed. Then the shooting broke out. Soon people were wounded and dying everywhere on the city streets. Mrs. Paraska, a skinny woman who lived nearby, was killed at high noon. At the time a couple of us were sitting with Grzesiek in the bushes, eating currants. Our eyes were set on a narrow path that ran along a field covered in tomato plants. Mrs. Paraska walked slowly along the path, carrying a heavy metal bucket. A German was firing at her from Woronicza Street. We saw her fall without making a sound. She lay on the ground. Blood oozed out of her forehead. Beside her lay the abandoned bucket, from which milk was dripping.

Afterwards, the rifle fire was joined by the thunder of artillery. German planes began dropping bombs. Our family took refuge from the air raids in a ground shelter behind the house. The shelter had a flat roof level with the ground and did not attract as much attention as Gizytcki's little palace that stood erect atop a cliff. We felt safe inside it, so the moment we heard the planes overhead, our entire family would run for the shelter. One time, a German pilot noticed some people running and dove in the direction of our shelter and dropped a bomb twenty metres from where we hid. My grandfather, upon hearing the detonation, died from a heart attack. That evening Uncle Michal, with Grandma Andula, carried Grandfather's remains to our home and laid him on the bed. As Andula gave him his final shave, his face looked frozen stiff. Afterwards she dressed him in a white shirt, a tie and a black suit. The next day, Uncle Michal dug a grave behind our house and we buried Grandfather among the currant bushes. Everyone, myself included, wept.

In the sky, there began to appear increasingly large numbers of German planes. Then a few dozen spitfire planes flew overhead, dropping food and ammunition in parachutes. Unfortunately, the Polish forces could not retrieve them: the Germans gathered the entire airlift. At night, the glow of fires rose above Warsaw. The fascists regrouped; a majority of their troops assembled on the outskirts of the capital. It was becoming increasingly difficult for the resistance to fight the enemy. In the end, General Komorowski announced the surrender. The insurgents abandoned their weapons and gave themselves up into the hands of the enemy. Germans were blowing up entire homes, churches and apartment blocks. They herded civilians around like cattle, through the burning ashes to the train station in Pruszkowo. From there, Poles were transported to labour camps in Rzeszy. My mother and I managed to escape. We spent an entire night in nearby bushes.

At dawn, we crept out and hopped a train bound for Krakow. After surviving countless misadventures, we eventually found ourselves in Stary Sacz, the home town of my mother's second cousin, Hela Mikula, a small woman with blue eyes. Her husband, a hunched-over peasant of medium height, was tilling the field. He had large veiny hands and a simpleton's mentality. Aunt Hela, though of noble origins (she even had a crested ring), had completely sunk to his level. She slaved over the property like an ox, tilling the field, milking cows, and feeding chickens. The day following our arrival the Mikulas wanted to put us to work. At that time, the Russians were approaching ever more quickly, encircling the German Army from several directions. The Germans, in retreat, blew up a nearby bridge. I was sitting on the window sill at the time, and the force of the explosion shattered the window, injuring my left eye. To this day, my sight is a little worse on that side.

During my recovery, I was often left on my own while my mother drove to Krakow to get flour that she would sell later for a much higher price in Stary Sacz. This activity was illegal, and it could have cost her dearly if she'd ever been caught, but it allowed her to pay off the Mikulas, sparing me the need to shred hay in the barn or feed the chickens. She even had the money to buy me paint for watercolours. A neighbour of the Mikulas, Mr. Zenek Pszczolka, admired my drawings. One day he brought over a doctor at his own expense.

"Sir," he said to the doctor, "you might give him some remedy for that eye. This young man is a budding Kossack. We must aid the artists in our midst."

"It's nothing serious," said the doctor. "That little scar on the lid will heal quickly and there will be not a single trace left behind." Then he examined my drawings. Nodding his head, he murmured, "The boy has talent."

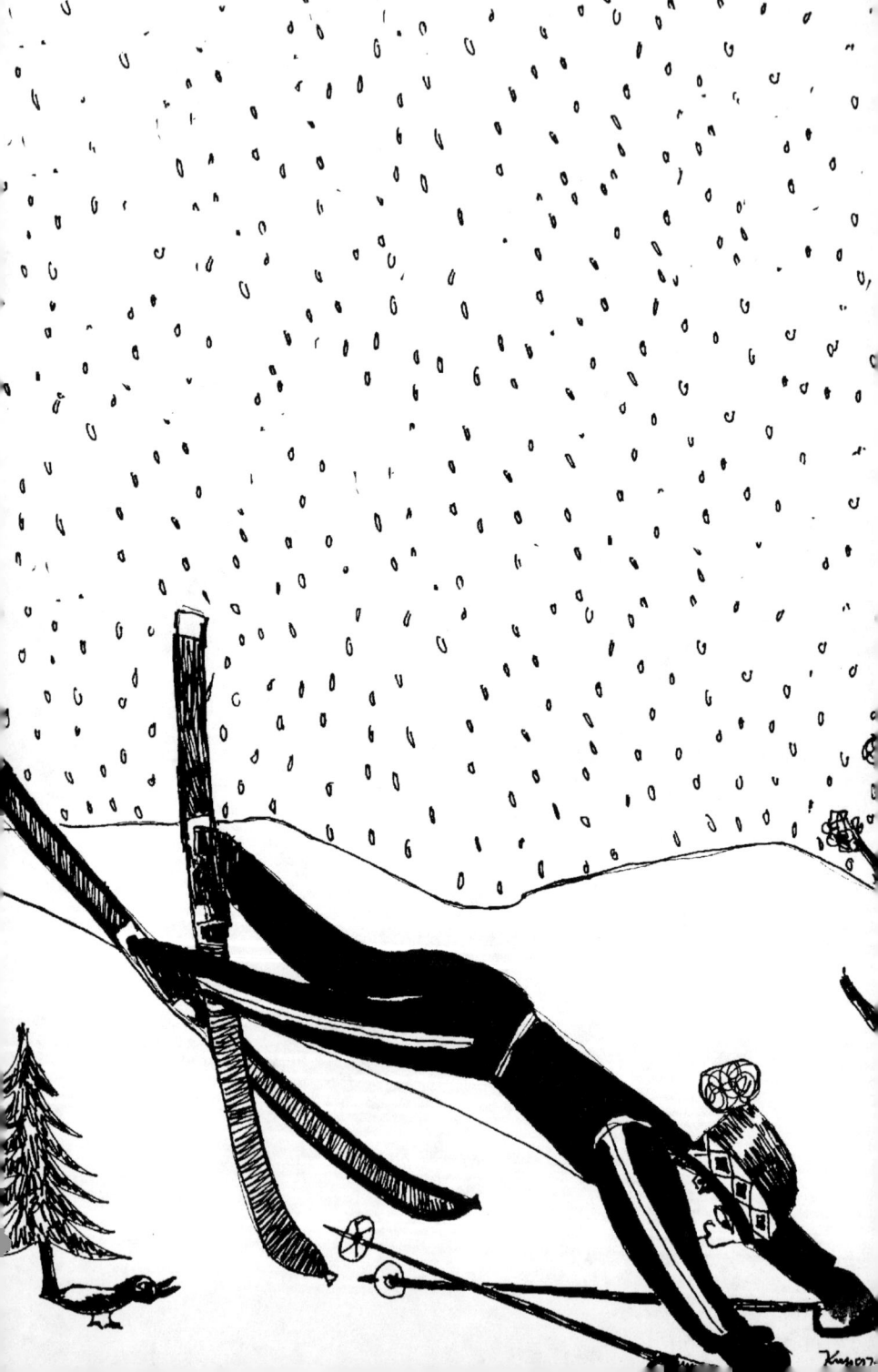

7

Relations with the Mikulas began to sour from the time that Zenek Pszczolka brought me a pair of skis. I remember scrambling on them to the summit of a fairly high mountain. I pushed away with the ski poles and swished downward. I had skied before back in Kolomyja, but only on flat terrain—except for the time I descended a steep barn roof and landed on my backside amongst snow-covered bushes. Now, as I accelerated down the slope, I was having difficulty standing up. I did not know then that in order to get down such a mountain I was supposed to regulate my speed with wide turns. No one had told me this, not my mother, who cared so dearly for my welfare, nor Uncle Michal, who had worked all his life in agriculture, nor Zenek Pszczolka, who had given me the skis in exchange for ten of my best drawings. So I sped down the mountain like a maniac. Terrified, I shut my eyes. Suddenly my right ski caught on a rock that was sticking above the snow and I shot up into the air like a cannon ball. Next thing I knew I was tumbling down the steep hill side doing somersaults. I felt a sharp pain in my knee. Then I came to a halt, having bumped into the trunk of a thick pine tree. One of my skis kept speeding downward and shattered on a wooden bridge. I gathered myself up.

"A fool is always graced with fortune," I muttered to myself as I hobbled home.

"I lost a ski but I didn't break a leg."

When she heard what had happened, Aunt Mikula proclaimed, "I'm not sorry for you at all. You're always wandering around where you shouldn't. It's a good thing you didn't break your neck on those so-called . . . skis."

Uncle Mikula came in from the cow shed. He had white paint on his face.

"It would be better for you to spend your time helping me paint the rabbit cage."

"With pleasure, Uncle, once my leg stops hurting."

The following day mother returned from Krakow. She had brought me a new sweater, which I needed badly because the Mikulas would not put glass in our bedroom window. It was always cold in there even under two quilts. In retrospect, I think that they kept the room cold on purpose to make us move out sooner.

We departed for Rzeszow in the spring. Everything was blossoming. The lilacs smelled sweet. The Germans were losing the war, retreating in panic from the Russian and Allied Armies. Rzeszow was where my encounters with girls began. It was there that I met Alina with the thick braid. I was a handsome boy and she fell hard for me. She even sang serenades under my window. One time I went with her to the river bank. We kissed each other there for several hours until our lips were swollen. I didn't know then that one could go further than that. All I did besides kiss her was run my fingers through her hair. Damn! I was such a romantic back then. Not until my encounter with

Zofia Diacinska, the stoker's wife, did I receive my education.

I discovered the Western Territories one day when three truckfuls of boys from our school drove to Zielona Gora. The teachers had enlisted everyone to work in the fields. The government of the newly formed Polish People's Democracy needed working hands, since Poles had settled in new lands previously populated by Germans. Empty homes stood there, gardens and pastures sown with wheat. We began to scythe it and make hay stacks. We worked in the field until nightfall. Then we ate an abundant supper complete with tomato juice and dessert. After the meal we had time to plunder the empty houses, where there were plenty of things to be found.

In one house I found a brand new green polka dot dress and a black hat for my mother, a pinstriped outfit for myself, a sewing machine, a hunting knife, a pair of high-heeled boots (in my mother's size), and a very beautiful parasol with large blue flowers. In one of the closets I discovered a set of silver utensils in a lovely ebony box decorated with a brass ornament. Professor Perdeus, who taught us Physics and Latin, had procured a piano from somewhere. "I will take it for my wife," he told Professor Wos, who was a major in Kosciuszko's army. Rumours circulated that he had ties to Soviet Intelligence. He collected mirrors in which he liked to examine himself. He took great pride in his face, especially his regular features and the thick dark hair that fell rakishly on his forehead. Despite his likeable Cary Grant exterior, Wos had sadistic tendencies, much like Miszka Baran. He liked to tear the wings off butterflies.

It was Wos's idea to allow some boys to return home alone, since he and Professor Perdeus wanted more space in the vans for their own loot. Thus seven of the forty students they had brought with them to work in the fields of the recaptured territories received an allowance for train fare and began walking to the station. Those among us who had the most loot, and I was one of them, were pushing it uphill in baby carriages.

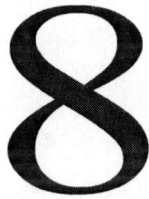

8

When we emerged onto the platform at the station, we were winded and hungry. There were three of us: Marek Kolodziej, Franek Kulesza and I. The other four boys were nowhere to be seen. Maybe they had had some trouble along the way. "The train for Rzeszow leaves at 8:30 p.m.," announced the fellow in the ticket booth. I emptied my things—three heavy packs wrapped in paper—from the baby carriage, placed them under my head, and covered myself with a sheepskin that I had found in an abandoned school. Marek set himself up nearby. The train arrived two hours late, its locomotive heaving from the strain of pulling forty cars. The front cars were full of Russian soldiers.

Heavily armed with bazookas and machine guns, they were bound for Berlin in order to strike the Germans a final blow. They were all boozed up and very loud. Some of them were singing to the sound of a harmonica. On the sly, we sneaked into the end wagon, sliding shut the heavy doors behind us. It must have been used to transport cattle. The entire floor was covered with straw. Immersed in the strains of music that travelled to us from the front of the train, I fell asleep.

I dreamt of a ballroom inside the Magistrate's Hall, where I went dancing every Saturday. Smiling pairs twirled in a waltz. I was dancing with a chair. Then a buxom girl with very beautiful green eyes appeared. "Wanna dance?" she asked, drawing near. Her hair smelled of spring. We danced together until midnight. When the clock struck twelve, the enormous oak doors of the ballroom parted soundlessly and twelve officers entered the hall. They were dressed in green uniforms featuring the Polish Eagle—without the crown and therefore resembling a pitiful hen. They talked together in broken Polish, weaving in Russian words. One lieutenant with a red face placed an arm on my shoulder.

"Allow me."

I ignored him completely, whisking Anielka to the opposite end of the room.

"Ubiju sobaku! "he thundered after me in a grizzly voice.

I turned around. The officer was aiming at me with a pistol. I laughed in his face. I do not know why, but when I looked into his crimson face under a four-cornered hat, a sinister mood came over me. I was not in the least afraid of him. I did not believe that he would have the gall to fire at me. His companion caught his arm. The music played on. "Red-face" found a different dance partner. He danced away, stomping boisterously.

It was then that the whistle of the locomotive brought me back to reality. Beside me, Marek was snoring. The smell of straw filled the compartment. Franek Kulesza slept with his jaw agape. The stuffed deer head he was bringing home for his mother was lying at his side. I turned over and went back to sleep.

Soon I was dreaming of my father. He had just stopped

playing his fiddle. My mother entered the room.

"Ignac, don't wander around in your underwear. Put something on. Stefa will be here anytime now."

"Stefa never comes to visit me," my father retorted.

My mother shrugged. "Everyone knows you've got a screw loose."

"And yours are all missing!"

They fought as usual and I ran to the garden. There I was in the process of picking black cherries and packing them in my mouth, when someone shook my shoulder. I opened my eyes . . . and found myself sitting in the dark compartment. The train stood still.

"We've been standing like this for two hours," said Marek. Franek was still snoring. I reached for the empty lemonade bottle and said, "I'm going to get some water."

I got off the train. Around me there was silence that was only periodically disrupted by the heaving of the locomotive. Close by the train station I found a well. Bending over it, I drank from a bucket of stale water. The next thing I knew, a Russian with an automatic pistol strapped to his chest appeared before me like a ghost. He grabbed my shoulder.

"Pogulajem?" he said, dragging me into the nearby bushes, his slanted eyes looking at me menacingly. I struck him in the face with such force that he collapsed on the muddy ground and I ran back to the train, leaving my water bottle behind. If he had been able to recover his senses, he could easily have shot me. When I told my friends what had happened, Marek laughed and said, "The Russian soldier—he wanted to fuck you." Unable to sleep, I tossed and turned from side to side until dawn, my stomach aching from the stinking water.

We arrived in Rzeszow at 9:00 a.m. When I got home, I

gave my mother the green polka dot dress and the black hat, both of which pleased her a great deal. My outfit was a bit too big for me. Mother said that she would shorten the sleeves and alter the pants. "Don't worry," she said. "I'll make you look elegant."

At Easter time we moved again, this time to Wroclaw, where we found an empty three-room house with a garden not far from the Odre River. Inside the kitchen drawers we found spoons, knives and forks. In the other rooms we discovered pots, a bed, a table and other furniture. Everything had been left by the Germans. Mother soon found a job in a grocery store, and I resumed my studies. At the high school on Poniatowsky Street, I enrolled in an accelerated curriculum and completed two grades in one year even though I did not apply myself. Most of my time was spent in cafés. It was there that I picked up smoking.

9

Nothing special went on in high school. The teachers did not demand too much—except for Ziobro, the mathematics professor who was endlessly on my case until I couldn't stomach any more of his sines and cosines. He had problems with his bladder: during his forty-five minute lesson he would have to leave for the washroom several times. When he returned, the blackboard would inevitably be covered with some "uncensored" little phrase that drove him up the wall.

One day Ziobro stopped turning up. No one knew what had happened to him. Mathematics lectures were taken over by Mrs. Krówczyñska, the choir teacher. Shortly afterwards I read in the paper that Professor Ziobro's body had been found in the Odre. He had apparently been shot in the head. The police conducted an investigation which at one point involved a visit to our school. The case was never solved.

Meanwhile, I fell in love with Wroclaw, with its medieval town square, old market, grand cathedral, opera and elegant hotels. The climate there was moderate, so spring arrived very early. In the summer I would go to Morskie Oko, the small lake whose beach was a popular meeting place for actors, dancers and opera singers.

It was there that I met Jerzy Michotek, the well-known singer; Teodor Szeptyski, the first tenor at the Wroclaw City Opera (he was a superb Jontek in Moniuszkowski's Halka); Tadeusz Szmid, the tall, thirty-something actor with a hawk nose and blue eyes who starred in the film Skarb Kapitana Martensa. My love interest at the time was Basia, a ballerina who used to give me tickets to the opera. Through her I met another Morskie Oko personality, the prima ballerina, Kalina Drozd. She had the best figure at Morskie Oko. I would have welcomed the chance to sleep with her, but tragically she had fallen for Maciek, a dancer with homosexual tendencies, and was completely under his spell. He would borrow money from her, always "eternally grateful," but would never give her in return anything other than the odd cheap bouquet of flowers. I would have been glad to rearrange his muzzle, but he was not cut out for a fight.

At the time I was less interested in painting than in film and singing. I would often look at my reflection in the mirror and see myself on the silver screen in a cowboy hat, galloping across the prairies on a prize stallion, gun in hand. After my encounters with the "stars" on the beach, I concluded that I looked better than most of them. If I decided to pursue a career in either film or singing, I thought, I would surely end up famous.

Thinking that singing might be the place to start, I enrolled in private lessons with Mrs. Krówczyñska. Her evaluation of my abilities, while not everything I could have wished, left me hopeful. "My son, you don't have the voice of a Woloszyn" she said, referring to one of her pet tenors, "but you present yourself well, so you'll be able to sing in an operetta." Returning once from a session with her, I heard a very low baritone voice singing in the park. It turned out to belong to Franek, a boy of about seventeen with a large head of closely cropped hair. He sat on a bench holding a huge red guitar under his chin. I sat down beside him, amazed by the heavenly quality of his voice. After a good talk, we ended up going for a beer.

Two days later I ran into him again. Accompanied by his guitar we sang the ballad about Don Quixote. Franek and I soon became great friends. I would improvise words to go with his melodies and he would show me the different chords on the guitar. He was the son of an organ player. A poor student, he had stopped going to school. In the mornings he worked in a butcher shop, and in the afternoons he sat in the park and sang. I brought him along once to a voice lesson with Mrs. Krówczyńska, but he didn't want to apply himself. Franek was as restless as the wind; he could not sit in one spot for very long.

As summer was ending that year, I spent my days at Morskie Oko. One day, after diving from the two-metre board into the deep water, I felt what I thought was the ground under my feet. When I pushed off to return to the surface, the ground—or whatever it was—sank under the pressure. As soon as I reached the surface I called out to the lifeguard, "something is swimming under my feet!" He responded by jumping into the water and then diving down to investigate. After a short while, he emerged with the corpse of a bald man in tow. "It's the engineer who drowned last week," he panted. After helping the lifeguard haul the decaying body to shore, I showered, dressed quickly, and left Morskie Oko.

The next day I left Wroclaw for Lodz to take a three-day entrance examination for the Theatre School. I was one of many candidates. When they finally called out my name,

I adjusted my hair and buttoned up my suit. In the examination room a tall, slightly hunched man with a powdered face looked at me inquisitively.

"Your name is Zbigniew Kupczynski?"

"That's right, Professor."

"Rector," he corrected me. "Why do you want to become an actor?"

Zelwerowicz's voice conveyed an air of affection, yet he examined me as if he wanted to find my weak side.

"I am interested in the theatre and even more so in cinema," I said.

"Do you like Krasicki's poem 'The Rabbit and the Wolf?'"

"I like it."

"Can you recite?"

"Certainly."

"Then go ahead."

We looked each other in the eye like opponents inside a boxing ring. I sailed through the verses effortlessly until I stumbled in one place. Zelwerowicz interrupted me with a cough. "Hmm, hmm."

"Can I continue?" I looked him straight in the eye.

"Never mind."

"He doesn't lack gall," said Winnicka, an aging actress with plucked eyebrows who was observing our interview.

"Gall isn't everything," noted Zelwerowicz. Then he told me to act out a small scene: "Imagine that you are in the street in Warsaw during the occupation as a member of the National Underground Army. Around the corner is a building where you are supposed to deliver a pamphlet. You are walking purposefully when, suddenly, you discover Germans at the gate. Instinctively, you retreat. Betraying nothing, you turn in the opposite direction, cross the street, and disappear."

I acted the scene as well as I could, which was apparently good enough for my judges, for I was accepted into the Theatre School to begin classes in October.

10

Urszula Bak had the looks of Greta Garbo. Unfortunately, she lacked her talent. She had been accepted to the Theatre School because of her connections: her aunt lectured there on the history of theatre. Urszula invited me to her room once, supposedly to read the script of Shakespeare's Romeo and Juliet. My thoughts, however, kept wandering to her full lips. Eventually I had to steal a kiss. Urszula welcomed my attention and drew me onto the sofa. Encouraged, I put my hand under her skirt. Urszula responded to my boldness by taking a magazine from under her pillow and beginning to read. "Honey, go ahead," she said. "I know sex is a beautiful thing." Her words hit me like a bucket of cold water. I jumped up and ran out of the room.

My acquaintance with Stanislaw Nadziewiedzki was more satisfying. He played mostly romantic leads in the Lodz Theatre. His style was not as pretentious as many of the more traditional actors. He spoke naturally, using the relaxed intonation and casual pronunciation of everyday speech. I cultivated a similar style, but Professor Zielinski, the diction coach, maintained that I spoke too fast and accused me of swallowing my syllables. No one at the school had heard of Marlon Brando at that time, so they didn't know that less-than-perfect enunciation was becoming acceptable. A few years later, Zbyszek Cybulski would be one of the first actors in Poland to use his natural voice on the silver screen. That is why Wajda ended up shooting several films with him.

My stay at the Theatre School lasted only one month, enough time to make me thoroughly sick of primed imbeciles speaking with artificial voices and lecturers looking like bureaucrats or Communist apparatchiks. In November I got off the train in Wroclaw once again. Wearing my green fedora and a long coat, I walked along streets covered in yellow leaves until I reached my mother's house. She was working at the toy store when I arrived. When she returned at the end of the day, she was not at all surprised to see me. "I knew that you wouldn't be able to stand it there for long," she said. "You were born a painter, not an actor." Then she began peeling potatoes for supper.

The next episode in my educational adventures took place at the Higher Academy of Fine Arts. A grey chateau on the banks of the Odre, it provided its students with a fine view of the cathedral. One day, a gentleman with a black mustache walked into the studio and threw an inquisitive glance at everyone. This man, Professor Geppert, had studied painting in Paris and knew more about art than all of the other lecturers combined. He was a fine teacher and, to his credit, did not belong to the Communist Party. The subject of most of his own work was horses, which he painted using a post-impressionist palette. His paintings could be found in many museums.

Geppert very quickly uncovered a talent in me. One day he had us produce still-life studies of fruit placed next to a bottle. Seven of us half-baked novices worked away at our easels, including Moniuszko, a fellow with a long scraggly mop top; Spider, a small hunch-back; Irka Klimek, whom we liked to call Tesciowa (Auntie); Sowa, a mountain man from Zakopane known as the Owl; Jan Kowalczyk, who copied nature with photographic accuracy; Krzysia Maliszewska; and myself.

Moniuszko was the first to finish. In his painting, which was marked by an elegant coolness, the fruit had delicate colours. Geppert nodded, saying, "Not bad. Not bad."

Krzysia Maliszewska had copied Moniuszko: the same colours, same lines, identical to the finest detail. "Where is your innovation?" said Geppert as he moved her easel a few metres away from her model. My friend Spider had painted the still life in black and white. "I don't like colours," he explained to Geppert, who simply nodded. Auntie was still working when Geppert stopped by her easel. She was having trouble with perspective. Her bottle was microscopic, smaller than the apple. The Owl had executed everything very carefully. On his bottle there was even a reflection of the sun that was streaming in from the window.

"Sir, what do you think of my work?" he asked Geppert. "I've tried to make everything as real as possible."

"It's too bad that you did not paint the smell of the apples," retorted Geppert ironically. "Copying nature doesn't achieve anything. Many have wasted themselves in the process. There must be an atmosphere present inside every painting. A well-painted canvas is like an open door inviting us inside the painting."

Finally, the gaze of our professor rested on my painting.

He stood for a moment with an open mouth. He took off his glasses, wiped them with a handkerchief, and said, "This canvas appears to possess no logic, but it is quite interesting."

"Blue apples!" called out Kowalczyk.

"Why not," replied Professor Geppert, "if the table is black?"

"Look, it's not black, but beige!" Kowalczyk protested.

"To me it is black," I said with zeal. "To me black is more in harmony with blue. When I look at nature, I often feel the need to set things in order, to paint it with greater contrasts. That is why I made the apples blue."

11

Some time later we began to paint Freda, a buxom woman in her forties who had a protruding belly and thick red hair that framed her sad face. A native of the recaptured territories, she spoke Polish very poorly. The only reason she had not been forced out of Wroclaw was that the city's mayor had taken a liking to her. When the mayor's wife and children turned up, however, their sweet liaison came to an end and Freda passed into the hands of Comrade Wrona of the Communist Party. When he tired of her, he found her work in a cafeteria where she swept the floors.

It was there that she met our Professor Rogal, who was immediately taken by her charms. He proposed that she work as a model at our school. That very evening he took Freda to the studio, sat her down naked on a wooden stool, and began to sculpt her. "I will make a fabulous work of art out of you," he told her, losing himself in her clear amber eyes. When the sculpting was done, they screwed on the studio floor. That is how Freda came to pose for us.

Professor Rogal, incidentally, was a mediocre sculptor who had only the Party to thank for the post of Professor at the Higher Academy of Fine Arts. He returned the favour by organizing a Communist Youth chapter in our school. Thanks to Rogal, the standard of teaching soon deteriorated by at least fifty percent. Party members who supported him sometimes boycotted the lectures of truly talented professors like Geppert. This allowed the school authorities to restrict the number of lectures they were allowed to deliver and increase the amount of Marxist drivel that could be given by the orthodox.

Rogal eventually became Rector. Under his rule anyone who, instead of painting in the naturalistic manner of social realism, used pure, "straight-from-the-tube" colours and simplified images, was automatically persona non grata. Students like me, Moniuszko or Leszek Kacma were headed for a collision with the apparatchiks.

The painters' workshops were festooned with plaster molds of hands, legs, even genitalia. I remember that Professor Dynia once ordered me to execute forty drawings of a plaster leg before allowing me to complete a fairly substantial canvas entitled "The Circus." He then showed my painting to the class and declared, "Kupczynski is a typical example of a person inflicted with the informalism of the decadent West. Instead of studying the true craft of Soviet artists like Riepin, he has been mesmerized by Picasso."

Moniek managed to defend me by saying, "I like the clown with the green nose."

"Such noses are strewn all over the carpets of Paris brothels," Dynia spat back, "and there is no place within Socialism for public houses. The worker is honest. He has a family, a wife, children. He has no need for whores."

"My painting depicts a circus, not a brothel," I said angrily.

"We have no need for circuses either. The worker visits the theatre," thundered Professor Dynia.

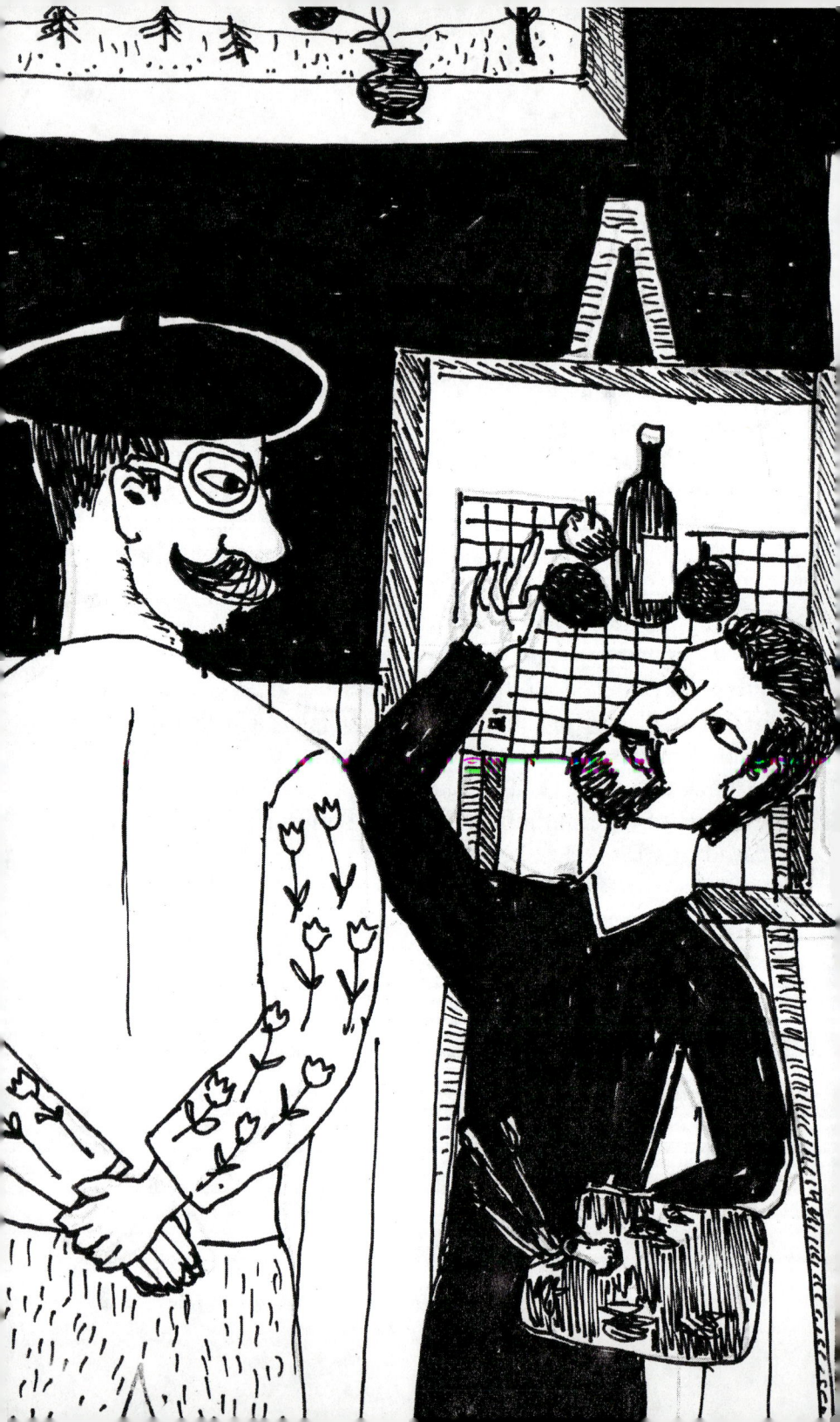

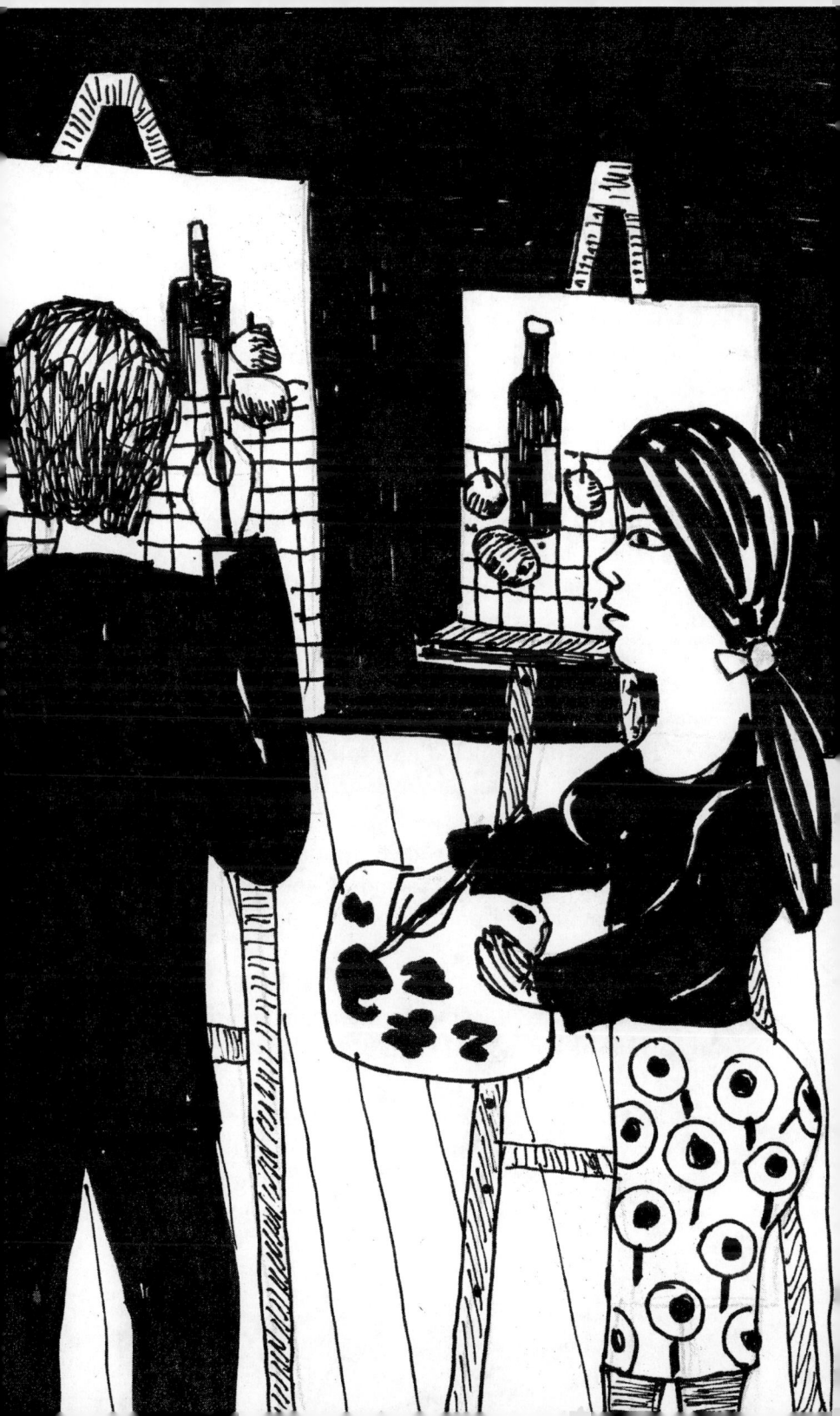

"I have yet to see a worker at the theatre," Spider remarked sarcastically, wiping his runny nose.

"Haven't you?" said Dynia, staring at my friend with his cross-eyed glare. "Well you will, let me assure you. We will educate them. Yes, we will!"

Everyone snickered. Professor Dynia turned red in the face, then quietly left the studio. The stale odour of his sweat lingered for a few more minutes, then dissipated.

Soon a new model by the name of Jasinski appeared at our evening drawing classes, a man with short legs and a long hairy torso. He stood there one day in his "birthday suit" staring out the window. It was autumn and the room was rather chilly. To warm himself, Jasinski moved closer to an iron radiator. Within minutes something unexpected occurred: his tiny member began to swell like a balloon. The first to notice was Krzysia, who let out a muffled cry and lowered her eyes in embarrassment.

"Oh dear!" cried out Tesciowa.

Then all of us, including Professor Pekalski, burst out laughing. Jasinski ran for the door, but Pekalski caught him by the arm.

"My dear man! You have nothing to worry about, it could happen to anyone standing too close to a heater. Please, resume your position on the stool. The lesson is not over yet."

"This is not my kind of work," said Jasinski. After dressing behind a screen, nervously humming a Strauss waltz all the while, he left, never to return.

Many months later, one Sunday afternoon during my fourth year, I saw Professor Geppert fishing from a bridge. Not having seen him in a long while, I filled him in on my progress and told him that I was beginning to despise our school.

"Everyone tries to find fault with me for the most insignificant reasons," I said. "These socialist-realistic tendencies in art are driving me crazy!"

"Then we are in the same boat. The authorities are displeased with my lectures, my paintings and my social life. If it weren't for my Anna's poor health, I'd spit at this God-forsaken school and earn a living from painting."

At that moment his colourful float disappeared under the water.

"Something's biting, sir."

Geppert reeled in an impressive fish. "Yes, well, patience sometimes pays off," he said as he took the fish off the hook.

Not long after this conversation, in 1952 to be exact, I left the Higher Academy of Fine Arts and obtained my certificate as a member of The Polish Association of Visual Artists, also known as the ZPA. At the same time something even more important happened: I met Renata, my future wife. She was standing at a tram stop. A beautiful girl with clear blue eyes, she looked at me with a winning smile on her face. She was in the company of a man of average height in a black bowler hat. When they rode away, I felt the inexplicable sadness of déjà vu. I had the feeling that somehow I had known this girl for years. Over the next days and weeks her smile pursued me in my dreams. One night she stood over my bed and said, "I have loved you from the moment that spring came to the city, when lilacs first began to blossom."

Shortly after this vision, I was awakened by a nightingale. I dressed hastily and walked to the kitchen. After making myself a cup of tea, I examined one of my unfinished paintings. Like much of the work I did at the time, its colours were not as vibrant as they are today. It reminded me of the sadness of a bird seeking a land of endless summer, a place where birds sing unceasingly. As I began to touch up the last tree in the garden on which nightingales were perched, I thought about the girl at the tram stop. I felt sure that we would meet again.

My intuition did not deceive me. We soon met and married and before long had a daughter we called Malgosia. She had a round chubby face, a tiny nose and Renata's blue eyes. My mother-in-law, Boba, an authentic Lithuanian princess, could not accept the fact that her daughter had betrayed her class by marrying a painter from a middle-class family that did not reek of money. In order to maintain control over our marriage, she invited us to share her two-bedroom apartment in Warsaw. So I left Wroclaw once again, this time for good.

My mother walked us to the train station. "Don't forget me," she said tearfully, slipping an envelope into my pocket. "Buy yourself some canvas and paints."

12

Soon after moving in with Renata's mother in Warsaw, I rode the #9 tram to Pulawska Street to visit my old neighbourhood. The Krolikarnia, where I had witnessed the beginnings of the Uprising, was untouched. Our house, popularly know as Gizycki's chateau, stood firm as before, although it seemed to have turned a little greyer since I had seen it last.

Looking into its windows, I felt sad. Afterwards I went to the spot where we had buried Grandfather, knowing full well that his body was no longer there, having been moved to the cemetery on Powaski by Grandma Andula and Aunt Lusia. His burial place put me in mind of Uncle Michal's death from stomach cancer. Then I thought of his daughter Wanda, my cousin, who had married Wlodek. At the time of their wedding I wore my hair long, combed over to one side. I told Wlodek that he should do the same. "That way people won't be able to see that your ears stick out," I said. Wlodek shook his head in protest and said, "What would the Party members say to such a hairdo?"

After leaving the house, I decided to walk through a field of tomatoes growing nearby. It was there that I heard a familiar voice call, "Zbyszek! Is that you?" Turning around

I saw Grzesiek Gurniaszek, one of the grocer's sons. He had grown up and become manly. We got caught up and I found out that he still called his brother Pyza (Chubby Cheeks), as in the old days. Thanks to him, I left the old neighbourhood in good spirits.

As I was riding the tram home, I thought of the life awaiting me at Renata's apartment on Narutowicz Square. Located on a top floor, with north-facing windows, it really belonged to her uncle Czes Zawotski, a former cavalryman in General Andersen's Army. Czes had fought on various fronts, including the deserts of North Africa, where he had been bitten by a tarantula. He was actually Renata's mother's cousin, but that had not stopped him from sleeping with her. The two of them drank heavily and smoked excessively. The walls of their room in the apartment were black from the smoke. The other room, where Renata and I lived with Malgosia, was cleaner but small and cramped.

I will never forget a New Year's Eve party at the home of the apartment. The table was spread with festive food and alcohol. The guests were dressed in their best finery. Boba's brother, Stanislav, had brought her flowers.

From the moment we met, Stanislav did not like me. Nor did he like my paintings. Stanislav was an amateur painter himself, painting portraits from photographs.

"How can you work so hard in the office while this bastard sits at home and does nothing?" he said to my wife. "You shouldn't be supporting him."

"It's none of your bloody business!" Renata snapped, angry at him for criticizing me in front of the guests.

Stanislav could not hold his liquor very well and after a few glasses of wine, he was quite drunk. He started to sing Christmas carols in a strange voice distinctly out of tune.

He sang so loudly that he woke Malgosia and she began to cry. Politely, I asked him to stop singing, but he responded with a dirty look and some fierce epithets about my mother. I was offended and returned his insult by calling him a fat pig. He raised his beefy fist to strike me, but I easily avoided his punch and gave him a shot from the left. My fist landed on Stanislav's chin and he fell heavily onto the carpet. He looked at me in fright and began to wail like a baby.

Unexpectedly, Boba came at me from behind, and unsheathing her long fingernails, she lashed out at my face viciously. Uncle Czes had to pull her off me.

"Don't touch this boy," he said. "He was just defending himself. Your brother deserved what he got. He started it."

Boba was not interested in listening to Czes's assessment of the situation. She took one more look at her weeping brother and then smacked Czes squarely on the face.

Meanwhile, the guests had been watching this domestic squabble in horror and when they had had enough, they grabbed their coats and left. The New Year's party came to an abrupt end. Fat Stanislav was the last to leave.

Boba locked herself in another room.

"Open up," yelled Czes angrily, shaking the door knob. Eventually he had to break the lock to enter the room. Immediately we heard Boba's scream followed by the sharp sound of her hand as it landed on Czes's face.

Czes came into the kitchen with blood oozing from wounds on his cheek. Applying a wet towel to his face, he sat at the table and broke down into tears.

"Look what she did to me! And I love her so much," he cried. He started to drink one glass after another as the candles burned on through the night. Eventually, Czes looked up from his drunken stupor and said to nobody in particular, "let's have some fun. Everyone deserves a little fun in the

New Year, don't you agree?"

Renata and I remained silent. He put on his brown coat.

"Where are you going, uncle? It's two o'clock in the morning," Renata said.

Czes looked at her through foggy eyes and slurred a response. "Where? To a whorehouse," he replied. "If your mother doesn't want me, somebody else will."

He left the kitchen. I turned off the lights and Renata and I went to bed, relieved that we could finally get some sleep. It was not to be. Soon the lights were on again as Boba stormed into the kitchen. She was dressed carrying two suitcases in her hands.

"I'm leaving this house forever," she announced.

"Where are you going, mother?"

"To Daddy. He is my husband. He has always helped in times of trouble. I will live on Saska Kepa with him. You can tell that bastard, Czes, he will never lay his hands on me again."

Renata wanted to get up from the bed, but I held her close and whispered, "don't move. It's not your concern. Besides, she's made her bed and now she has to lie in it."

And so Boba left. For the next few days, peace and quiet reigned in the house. Presently, Czes reappeared sporting a black eye.

"How are you kids?" he asked softly. "You know, I really don't mind if you stay in my home."

We were taken aback by his generosity. The next day Czes went to work. Renata also had to go to the office and so I was left alone in the apartment with Malgosia. This arrangement continued for a while, and seemingly things were back to normal.

Then late one evening there was a sharp knock on the door. Czes opened the door and found two officers of the

Secret Police standing on the threshold. They ordered Uncle Czes to get dressed and escorted him from the apartment. During the Occupation, Uncle Czes had belonged to the right wing of the underground army and that was enough of an indictment for the Communists to arrest him.

After his arrest Renata's mother came back home. She was hired as a typist in the same office where Renata was employed, which left me with more room to move. Malgosia and I were left to ourselves from nine in the morning until four in the afternoon, free to do as we pleased. On the home front, trouble began when Boba quit her job and stayed around the apartment most of the day. The complaining started again.

"You don't do anything around this place! Why don't you make yourself useful?" she screeched.

I changed Malgosia's diapers, fed her her bottle, and when it was sunny outside, I put my little girl in a carriage and took her to the park. I always had my sketchbook with me so I could draw her in different positions and in different settings. I was fascinated by her tiny figure, her chubby face and turned-up nose, her huge grey eyes, the thick white curls that surrounded her face. When she laughed, I would paint her in yellow or orange. When she cried, I used blue. Soon our small room was full of her portraits.

One day around noon someone knocked on the door. When I opened it I beheld Elzbieto Kosicka, a friend from the Polish Association of Visual Artists. She had brought along a guest from France, a famous Parisian painter who was a friend of Pablo Picasso. His name was André Pignon. He looked around at my paintings, nodding his head. In the end he said something in French. Elzbieto translated: How is he able to paint such colourful images in this dark place where there is so much junk and no proper light? Subsequently he

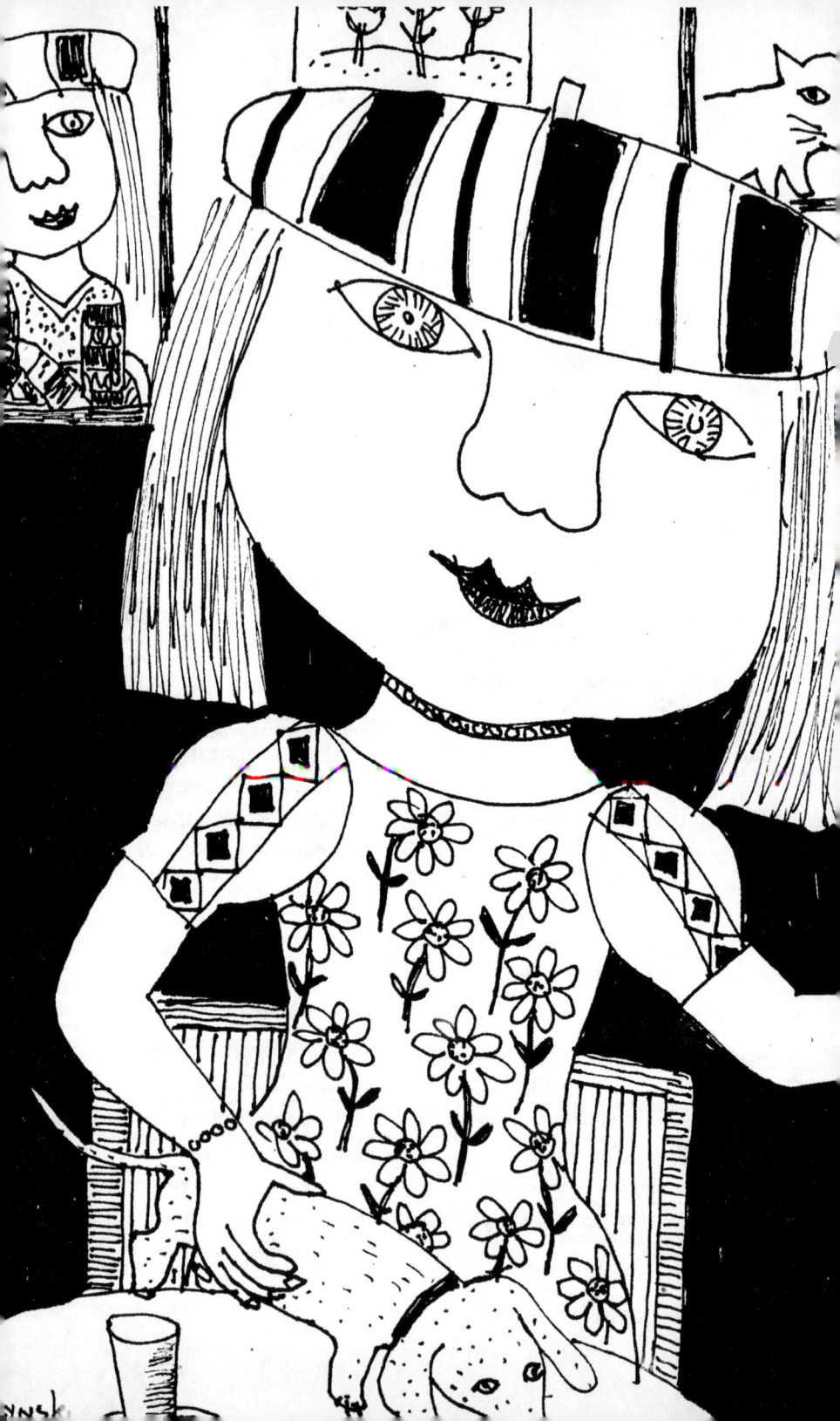

must have made similar comments to Party members, for shortly after this visit I mysteriously received a substantial upgrade in my living conditions.

About this time I met Iga at a meeting of the Art Association. She had long blond hair and the same startling blue eyes as Renata. Iga asked me if I would pose for her. I hesitated. Being on the other side of the easel would be a new experience for me.

"I don't know," I said. "I am a painter myself, and besides, I am a married man."

"Are you scared to come to my studio?" she asked coyly, showing beautiful white teeth.

The next afternoon found me knocking at her door. Iga greeted me with a smile. She was dressed in a white blouse and blue jeans. I entered her studio, a one-bedroom apartment facing the River Vistula. She made me a drink and then sat down in a rocking chair to appraise her reluctant model. Meanwhile, I looked about the apartment, taking note of her work. I was not very impressed.

She started making sketches of my face. Iga liked to listen to music while she worked. The soothing strains of the classical music relaxed me and soon I was comfortable as her muse.

I started visiting Iga regularly. After several sittings, she finished my painting. I didn't like it at all.

"I'm not satisfied either," she said. "I have to do another piece."

"Would you mind if I painted too?" I asked.

She set up another easel for me in the studio. "It's a very good idea," she said, watching me.

I painted a still life which was on the table while she continued to paint me.

"The portrait of a painter with brush in hand," Iga announced, examining her work.

Comparing the finished products, I could see that my piece had far more character than hers. In fact, she was quite a mediocre artist by every stretch of the imagination. However, she had redeeming graces; she was very nice to me.

One day after we had drunk a couple of bottles of wine, I fell asleep. When I woke up a few hours later, I discovered that I was in her bed, completely naked. Iga was lying beside me also undressed. Fully awake, she watched me seductively like a cat.

"You got quite drunk," she said, stroking my chest.

In the natural course of events, we made love. What else could I do? It was raining outside which gave me the perfect excuse to succumb to Iga's charms. It felt good being under the blanket with her warm body close to mine. Moreover, sex with Iga was without the tension that accompanied my lovemaking with Renata. At home it seemed that our every move, even in bed, was monitored by the countess. Not to mention Malgosia, who was never far away. In fact, she often watched from the small bed as Renata and I made love.

Being intimate with Iga did not make me feel guilty; however, I lied to Renata about whom I had been with.

"Where have you been?" Renata asked as I walked into the kitchen.

"I was visiting another painter," I answered.

"Who is he?" she asked.

"His name is Zak," I lied. "He has a studio downtown and I can paint with him. He likes my work."

"Would you rather work there than at home?" Renata asked.

"You know I can't use oils here because of Malgosia.

There, I can do anything," I explained.

I went a couple of more times to Iga, but every time I came home, I began to like myself less and less for the lies I had to tell. Sex with Renata became a burden. Something was wrong. She often avoided making contact with me in bed and it made me angry. One day when she refused my advances, I became furious.

"Okay, suit yourself," I sneered. Then, I told my wife about Iga. To my utter amazement, she began to laugh.

"I know all about it," she said.

"How?"

"That's my secret." Renata remained silent.

I didn't know what to say. In my confused state, I offered, "If you want, I'll stop seeing her and paint here."

"You know Malgosia can't be near the smell of oils. It's bad for her."

Reluctantly, I went back to Iga's to work. While painting one afternoon, we were disturbed by a knock at the door. It was Renata.

"I'm Zbigniew's wife," she announced, "and the mother of his child. I know that you two are intimate with each other. You can have him if you want. It would probably be best if he took his belongings and moved in with you. That's all I have to say. Good bye and good luck."

Renata turned to go. I followed her out the door calling after her, "Wait, Renata!"

She was walking very fast, but I caught up to her. She was wearing only a light dress in the cool autumn air. Protectively, I tried to put my jacket around her shoulders, but she rebuffed my efforts. My jacket was thrown on the street.

"Leave me alone," she cried bitterly.

Dying September leaves stuck to the fabric of my jacket. Stooping to pick it up, I didn't walk any farther. I just stood there as the blood emptied out of me, watching her form grow smaller and smaller in the distance. She turned the corner and was gone.

Not knowing what to do with myself, I went into a restaurant and ordered a beer. Several drinks later I recovered my equilibrium and I made my way home. The first thing I saw when I opened the door was a suitcase. My whole life had been stuffed into one bag.

"Take your things and go," she said.

Boba was standing beside Renata, wordlessly staring.

"What about her?" I asked motioning to the sleeping Malgosia.

"Don't worry. She'll be alright," Boba snapped. Turning to Renata, she added, "I've always known he was not for you."

There was pain on Renata's face. "Do you really want me to leave you?" I asked quietly.

"Yes, I do."

I took one last look at my sleeping child before picking up my suitcase from the floor. Hot tears stung my eyes as I struggled to hold them back. I couldn't let my wife and her mother see me cry. I left without another word.

Iga was cooking when I arrived at her studio. She offered me a beer. There was a hint of triumph in her voice.

"The wardrobe is over there. Why don't you unpack your things and put them away?" she suggested. "I even have a toothbrush for you."

I sat on a chair and stared blankly out the window. Seeing the sadness leeching my face, Iga came over to me and gently kissed my cheek.

"Don't worry. We'll have a great time together. You know what we are going to do tomorrow? We are going to paint a church," she announced brightly.

"What church?"

Iga explained her latest commission to me, which involved the restoration of a church. She showed me the photographs. It was a small eighteenth-century church in Kelpino close to Gdansk.

"The local priest wants me to repaint everything inside. The job is worth a lot of money," Iga said. She brought out a black portfolio from her closet.

"These are my projects," she said.

Iga had never shown me this work of hers before. She surprised me. The portfolio contained a big composition featuring the twelve apostles at the Last Supper.

"I'm going to paint these saints. It will be a great piece." Then, turning to me, she added, "there is also a ceiling which you will work on. Have you ever done anything like this before?"

"Never. I've only ever done paintings."

"Never mind. You'll have no problem. I know that you're very talented. We will leave Warsaw tomorrow at ten o'clock in the morning, alright?"

"Okay," I said, not knowing what else to do. I really didn't care about anything anymore.

Iga bought two train tickets. We arrived in the small

13

village of Kelpino at seven o'clock in the evening. The church stood alone like a beacon of light in a green valley. Father Piotr was waiting for us. He gave Iga a room in his home while I was quartered in a small nearby hotel.

Father Piotr invited us for supper at his home. Also present at the meal was Father Piotr's rather attractive assistant, Veronica. Looking at her voluptuous figure, I wondered whether she offered the priest more than just housekeeping services. In any case, we enjoyed a pleasant meal together. After clearing the dishes from the table, Veronica joined us for a stroll over to the church. The moon, standing at attention like a white knight, cast a glow over the building on which we were to work.

Inside, I was astonished by the poor condition of the altar and the old mural on the wall. It contained a very shoddy rendition of the twelve apostles.

"This old mural was done about ten years ago by a local artist who is dead now," explained the priest.

"What happened to him?" I inquired.

Nonchalantly the priest replied, "He met with a car accident."

The ceiling of the church had been constructed with

big, heavy beams. The dark hues added a certain gravity to the atmosphere of the church.

"These beams should be decorated in some way," said Father Piotr to Iga.

Pointing at me, Iga answered the priest, "That will be his job."

I soon discovered that Iga possessed a sharp business acumen. Skillfully, she negotiated an estimate for the job and drew up a contract that was quickly agreed upon by both sides. For our efforts, she would earn two hundred thousand zloty, a highly attractive sum. Iga offered me twenty percent.

In short order Iga went to Gdansk to order some art supplies. She asked me to stay behind and think about the design we were going to execute on the ceiling. I agreed to her demands thinking all the while that Iga was not as soft as I had previously thought. She returned from Gdansk the next morning with a whole truckload of art supplies in tow. This was a highly efficient woman.

"You are responsible for the ceiling," Iga told me. "You can do whatever you want, but I recommend a different type of ornamentation for each beam. The colours, however, should all work together. Agreed?"

"Fine," I said.

I jumped onto the ladder and climbed up, carrying in my hand paints and brushes. I opened my first can of paint to discover a clear, cerulean blue staring back at me. With swift strokes, I painted blue tulips with green leaves on my first beam.

Stepping back to appraise my work, I asked Iga, "What do you think?"

"Hmmm. Not bad."

I opened another can of paint. This time it was red. I

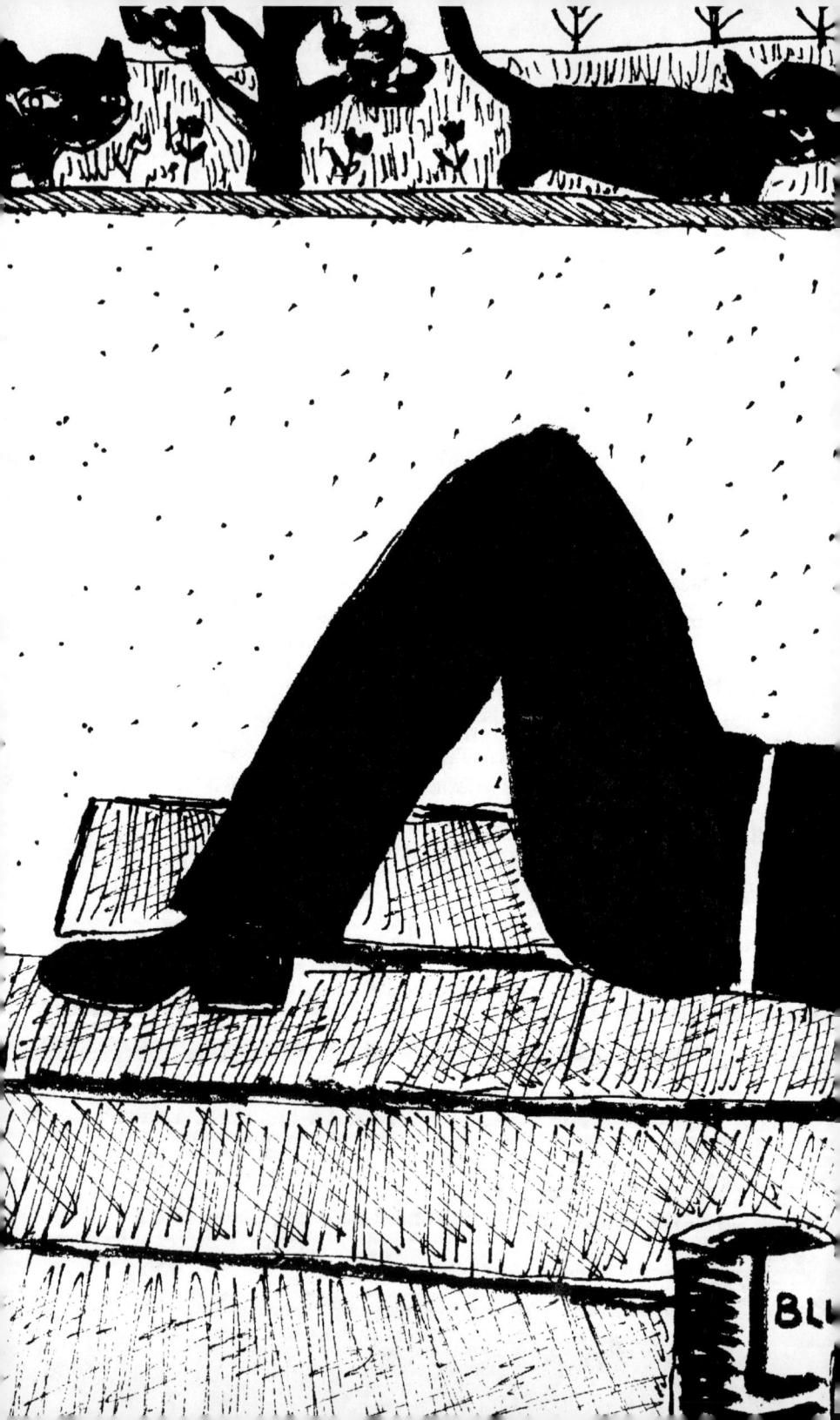

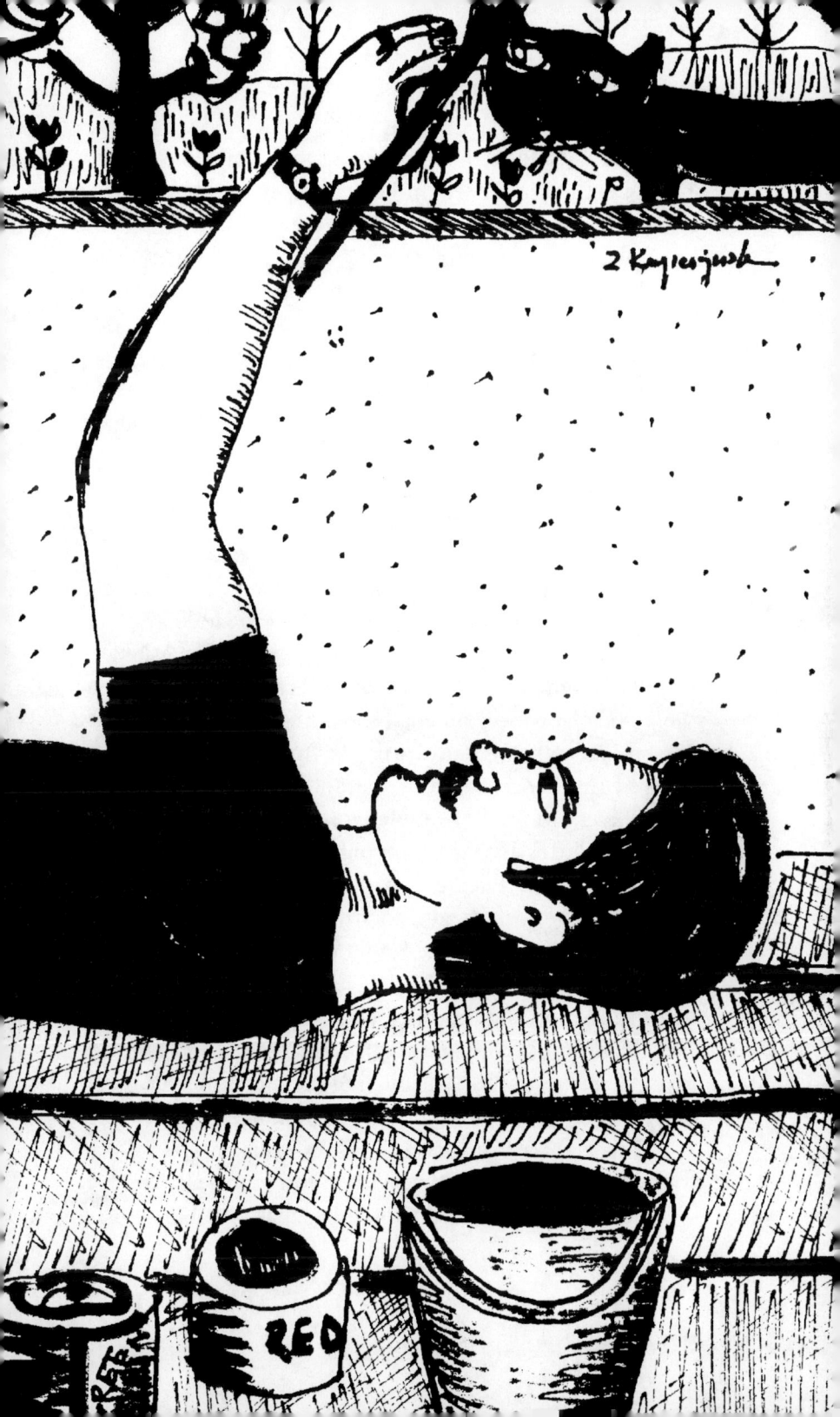

announced, "The next beam will be red, white and violet."

Butterflies suddenly flitted across my mind. I opened a can of yellow paint and I painted a cornfield.

"Everything is too yellow," I muttered to myself. I added some blue cornflowers. I climbed down the ladder so I could see what I had done. I laughed out loud at the riot of colours on the beam.

Hearing my laughter, Iga descended the platform from which she was working. She happily approved. In our gaiety, we didn't notice that Father Piotr had entered the church.

I told the priest, "I'm going to cover this ceiling with many plants and animals. When your parishioners look upwards, they will really see Paradise and smile."

Father Piotr answered back, "My son, you forget that my folks come to church to pray and not to smile."

"What's wrong with praying with a smile?" I asked.

I had opened twelve cans of different paint and so far, twelve beams were painted. Trees, mushrooms, butterflies, flowers and other fanciful images from the natural world covered the beams. Like a marauding army, I had conquered every inch of available wood space.

Meanwhile, Iga was having some trouble with the placement of the twelve apostles on the wall mural. Her colours were too delicate, looking somewhat muted and dingy in comparison to the bright colours I had used on the ceiling.

"I think you should tone down your colours by mixing them. Don't use the paint directly from the can," Iga advised, unsuccessfully disguising the pique in her voice.

I ignored her. I would never abandon my bright colours.

"Don't worry, my son. Follow your intuition," the priest said to me. "I know it will all turn out well."

Then Father Piotr did something that sent Iga into fits

of mortification. He advised her to change the brown dress of one of the saints to green. Iga recoiled and told the priest that she knew how to handle colours without any gratuitous advice from him. Father Piotr shrugged his weary shoulders and walked away without saying a word.

He came back a few hours later and reiterated his point, "You know, green would be much better for those apostles. And don't forget that they were from Nazareth and the sun should be reflecting off their shoulders."

Iga was not amused, and she began to see me as the cause of her discontent.

As we continued our work in the church, the tension grew between Iga and me. She seemed to be paying more attention to my ceiling than she was to her mural. It was the first time I had ever done this kind of work, but I felt as if I had been doing it all my life. I was really enjoying myself.

Three days later there was an accident in the church. Iga slipped off the platform and plunged to the hard stone floor below. I thought that she had killed herself. I scampered down from my perch to where she was laying, pools of blood staining the stone floor. In a state of shock, I ran to get Father Piotr.

We ran back to where Iga had fallen. To my great relief, Iga had revived and she was moving ever so slightly. She was alive, but in great pain. Father Piotr gently lifted her from the floor and placed a pillow beneath her head. She looked pale and drawn against the bloodstained white cloth. He called an ambulance and Iga was transported to the hospital.

I was beside myself with worry. It was only the day before that she had been laughing, full of life and vitality. Now I feared for her life.

"I will pray for her," said Father Piotr gravely.

It wasn't long before Father Piotr and I received news from the hospital. Iga had broken her leg and there had been some injury to her head, but her condition was not critical.

Later in the evening, there was another call from the hospital. "They reported that her condition had improved and she had even spoke a few words.

"God has taken care of His child," Father Piotr intoned while raising his eyes to the ceiling in silent prayer.

Then suddenly in a serious voice he asked me, "could you finish the mural of the apostles that Iga was working on? According to the contract we drew up, it really must be finished soon. If she can't do the job, somebody else has to do it. That would be you."

I hesitated before answering, "I don't know. It's her work."

"You can paint the apostles in brighter colours. I feel very sorry for the poor girl, but on the other hand, if she hadn't had the accident, the altar would have ended up looking terrible."

With sudden contempt, I looked on the face of the man who was supposed to be a priest and a primal urge to strike him came upon me. His proposition had greatly offended. I braced myself and shuffled off to resume my work on the ceiling. Working like a man possessed, I pondered the priest's offer.

Presently, the hospital called with a request for me to visit Iga. When I walked into her room, I was aghast to see her bound up in a leg cast and a brace around her neck. However, colour had returned to her cheeks and my worry quickly disappeared. She inquired in a steady voice, "How is the work going?"

I told her that the ceiling was almost finished and that I

would probably be finished at the end of the week. "After that, I will be working on your mural," I added.

Nonplussed, she replied, "You don't have to do that. Professor Gawel is coming to Kelpino to take care of that. He's a good friend of mine."

"That's great," I said to Iga, "because I didn't want to change your colours."

"What do you mean?" Iga responded guardedly, a sharp glint in her blue eyes.

I told her that Father Piotr had asked me to change the colours on the apostles, but I had refused.

If Iga hadn't been so encumbered, she would have hit the roof. "Good," Iga replied. "That bastard doesn't know anything about art."

"Maybe so, but he is the one who's paying us," I said curtly.

A worried look came over her face. A thought crossed my mind that our friendship was coming to an end. We spoke for a short while and she asked me if I wouldn't mind leaving.

"I have to get some sleep," she said. "I'm very tired."

I kissed her on the cheek and left.

Professor Gawel arrived three days later with a young, freckled assistant. While they were beginning to work on Iga's mural, I climbed down from my platform to introduce myself. Professor Gawel and his assistant looked upwards to appraise my work on the ceiling.

"Why do you use such bright colours?" asked the professor. "Why not?" I replied tersely. "I always use bright colours."

A conspiratorial look was exchanged between the two men. Later in the evening the assistant came to me.

"Your ceiling is so vibrant that it could kill the mural,"

he said.

I told him that it was too late for me to change anything. "Besides," I explained, "Iga saw my work from the beginning and she liked it."

"The poor girl. She must not have realized what she was doing," replied the assistant. Then he asked me, "How long have you known Iga?"

"Long enough," I answered.

The next day during lunch Professor Gawel asked Father Piotr what he thought of my work.

"I love it. His sense of colour is marvelous," enthused the priest.

"That's too bad," said Gawel. "His ceiling will kill the altar."

"Not necessarily," countered Father Piotr. "You should use brighter colours too. Nobody likes greys and browns in a church."

Professor Gawel was not to be rebuffed. "What do you know about art? This kind of work calls for a very careful use of colours—especially in a church."

"Professor, you'll recall that Michelangelo used bright colours in the Sistine Chapel," said the priest. "Iga is not Michelangelo. It's unfortunate, but somebody has got to tell the truth. I am very proud of my church and I want my parishioners to feel happy when they see the illustrations on the walls. The ceiling is smiling and the altar is crying. It's all so incongruous. Why can't you see this?"

Nobody could agree on anything. Over the next three days I tried to complete the ceiling while the professor finished off the mural, adding some yellow in an effort to appease Father Piotr. The end result was terrible. Even the holy visage of Jesus grimaced in being part of the distasteful rendition of the Last Supper.

Finally the mural was finished and the professor departed from Kelpino, leaving me alone with my ceiling. I painted the remaining beams with an aquamarine cat, a tree and two daisies. I repeated the series over and over from one end of the beam to the other. When I finished, I climbed down to view what I had done. I smiled.

Inspired by my success, I opened a fresh can of paint and frenetically began to paint my next subject, a red dog. A green frog and two tulips followed. Again, I repeated these images the length of another beam. On the last beam, I painted many different kinds of flowers. To improve the effect, I added a violin between each flower. My inspiration was complete.

"The masterpiece is done," I announced to no one in particular.

On Sunday the parishioners streamed into the church and took their usual places in the pews. As he did every week, Father Piotr prayed at the crucifix at the altar. Suddenly a small boy staring up at the ceiling began to meow like a cat. Other children in the church chimed in. A joyful cacophony of meows and barks sounded in the hallowed halls of the church.

"Meow, meow, woof, woof!" Even the sound of a frog was heard among the melange of animal sounds. "Ribbit, ribbit."

All mayhem broke loose. "Cats are in the church! Cats are in the church!" cried an hysterical woman.

By now, all eyes were on the ceiling as the wailing of the children continued. Finally, Father Piotr looked up and his face turned all shades of red.

"Silence, please! Silence!" he appealed. "Our artist made a mistake. We don't need cats on the ceiling. He will eradicate them, I assure you."

Reluctantly, I had to undo what I had done. The next day with a heavy brush in hand, I replaced all the cats with trees. My work at the church finally came to an end. So did my relationship with Iga.

When I returned to Warsaw, I went back to the small flat at Uncle Czes's at Narutowicz Square where Renata was living with Malgosia. Knowing that I had split with Iga and that I had earned some money from painting the church, Renata took me in again. She needed me as a babysitter because she wanted to continue working at the office. Our sexual relations remained strained.

Better times soon came my way, at least in part because of changes in Poland's leadership. President Bierut died during a visit to the Soviet Union, where he had been summoned by Stalin himself. He was brought back to Warsaw in an oak coffin. His successor was Wieslaw Gomulka, whom we called Gomula. He promised a better life and greater freedom in the Arts.

A national exhibition was being mounted at the Zahenta Art Gallery, and so I took two of my paintings to them. One of the pieces was a portrait of Malgosia in green and the other was of cherry trees in blue. The jury accepted them and my work was hung in the most prominent state gallery in the country.

Positive reviews of the exhibition appeared in the Warsaw Press. For the time being at least, the old masters of Socialist Realism were out of favour. Warsaw wanted to honour its new, young, heroic artists—people like Gierowski, Jas Lebenstein, Izaac Celniker, Nowosielski, Hasior, and myself. Our works began to be featured in the national galleries, and we were involved in many conferences and television interviews. In one such interview, I stood in front of the camera and swiftly painted my little Malgosia. This footage of me working was later shown from time to time on Polish television. Combined with reviews of my work in the press, this exposure turned me into something of a celebrity. Everywhere Malgosia and I went, people began to recognize us. "Look," they would say, "there goes the painter and little Malgosia from TV."

The Association of Visual Artists awarded me a brand new studio in the town in Warsaw. My first one man show was at the writer's club on Krakowski Przdmiescie. I presented twenty canvasses. Patrons would sit at their tables, coffee in hand, and discuss my work. At this stage I was doing a realistic type of art though the style was primitive and unique in character. My vision of the world manifested itself in simple bold colours.

14

About half a year later I received a scholarship from the Ministry of Art and Culture to study in Paris. The award did not reflect the Ministry's appreciation of my talent, but rather its desire to get me out of the country. This would put an end to my criticism of Party members who had abandoned Socialist Realism as soon as the shifting political winds made it safe to do so. After the Third National Exhibition, several members of the old guard had joined the circle of young rebels and begun to paint in the style of Picasso. One of them was professor Kobzdej, the author of a great piece of kitsch entitled "Podaj Cegle" (Pass the Brick). Another was Wojciech Fangor, who had gained recognition from a piece of socialist propaganda entitled "Matka Koreanka" (A Korean Mother). Even Professor Brona, the head of the Cultural Council, turned from the propaganda of the Soviet painter Riepin to the cubism of Picasso. I took great pleasure in criticizing these chameleons and others like them.

Even so, I welcomed the chance to go to Paris. Soon after news of the scholarship came, I pulled my best canvasses off their stretchers, withdrew my sixty-thousand-franc award from the bank, and left Warsaw for France. My travelling companion was Zbyszek Siemaszko, who like me had received a scholarship from the Ministry. Driving in his new Peugeot, we sped across the Polish countryside, carrying in our trunk a good supply of vodka and sausages we planned to sell in Switzerland in order to cover our travelling expenses.

When we arrived in Bern, a large rather ugly city, we checked into a clean downtown hotel. That evening we went to a restaurant to eat something and to sell our contraband. Our plan was to stimulate demand for it by distributing a limited amount of vodka and sausage free of charge. One of the Czechs we treated in this way, a fellow by the name of Ivan Swoboda, offered to introduce us to someone who would be willing to sell us chewing gum at warehouse prices. Judging that this commodity would bring us a healthy profit later on in our travels, we took him up on his offer—and soon found ourselves in the company of an undercover cop. Fortunately, he liked our vodka and sausage so much that he lost any desire he might have had to arrest us for illegal trade. "You have to be careful," he told us, then gave us the address of the chewing gum merchant, from whom we bought large quantities which we stuffed under the seats of the car. "We have more luck than brains," I said to Siemaszko as we resumed our journey.

It was a damp and misty evening when we arrived at the Austrian border. A man in a green uniform with an automatic slung over his shoulder asked us if we had anything to declare.

"Nein," said Zbyszek.

The guard didn't buy it and told us to step out of the car. Out of nowhere, two other uniformed fellows appeared.

One examined our passports and the other two turned all of our stuff inside out. They discovered and then confiscated our gum. One even wanted to retain my paintings.

"*Kunst* is not subject to customs," I reminded him.

We managed to hang onto the paintings. Even so, as we drove to Vienna, we were not in the best of spirits.

"I bet you the bastards are chewing our gum," I said to Zbyszek. "They always keep the loot."

"I wouldn't begrudge them their small pleasures," he said philosophically. "Would you want to be a customs official?"

We soon found ourselves in Vienna, the city of Mozart and Beethoven and Johann Strauss, which welcomed us with its murky alleys, its narrow cobblestone streets, and its horse-drawn carriages that shared the road with Volkswagens and Mercedes.

In some square near a fountain, an enormous poster displaying a naked man with a curly mop of hair had been plastered onto the grey fence. His beard, of a reddish tinge, covered his belly and genitalia. The bottom of the poster read:

FRIEDENREICH HUNDERTWASSER
AUSTELLUNG, Gallery 3.

"Let's go see his paintings," I said to Zbyszek. "I'm curious to see how a person with such a beard paints."

We parked our car near a church not far from the gallery. The opening was just under way. The painter (the man featured in the poster), dressed this time, was wearing a black shirt with large red circles, short pants that left his hairy calves exposed, red leather sandals and a gold medallion.

The paintings on the gallery walls were strange; never

in my life had I seen anything like them. There were vibrant spirals, like enlarged fingerprints, inside which life was burning. Zbyszek put his arm on my shoulder and said, "I'm going to get the camera."

I approached Hundertwasser and introduced myself, showing him a colour photograph of one of my portraits of Malgosia. Hundertwasser regarded it with curiosity. When Zbyszek returned, he took a photo of Hundertwasser and me. Then the three of us started drinking red wine.

When we were all good and drunk, Zbyszek and I returned to our car. Before we could leave, Hundertwasser came over with a girl hanging on each arm. He wanted to see my paintings, but something about him irritated me. Maybe it was the way he swayed in his drunkenness, or maybe it was those two stupid girls gaping at him as if he were some sort of god. I told Zbyszek to drive away. I had all that I could take of these people, and my head was beginning to ache from all the red wine. Zbyszek worked his way expertly through the city traffic and we were soon sailing down the highway toward the Swiss border.

"Why did he irritate you so much? Because he can paint well?" Zbyszek laughed.

I was silent. As I drifted to sleep I looked with a dreamy gaze at the outline of the mountains.

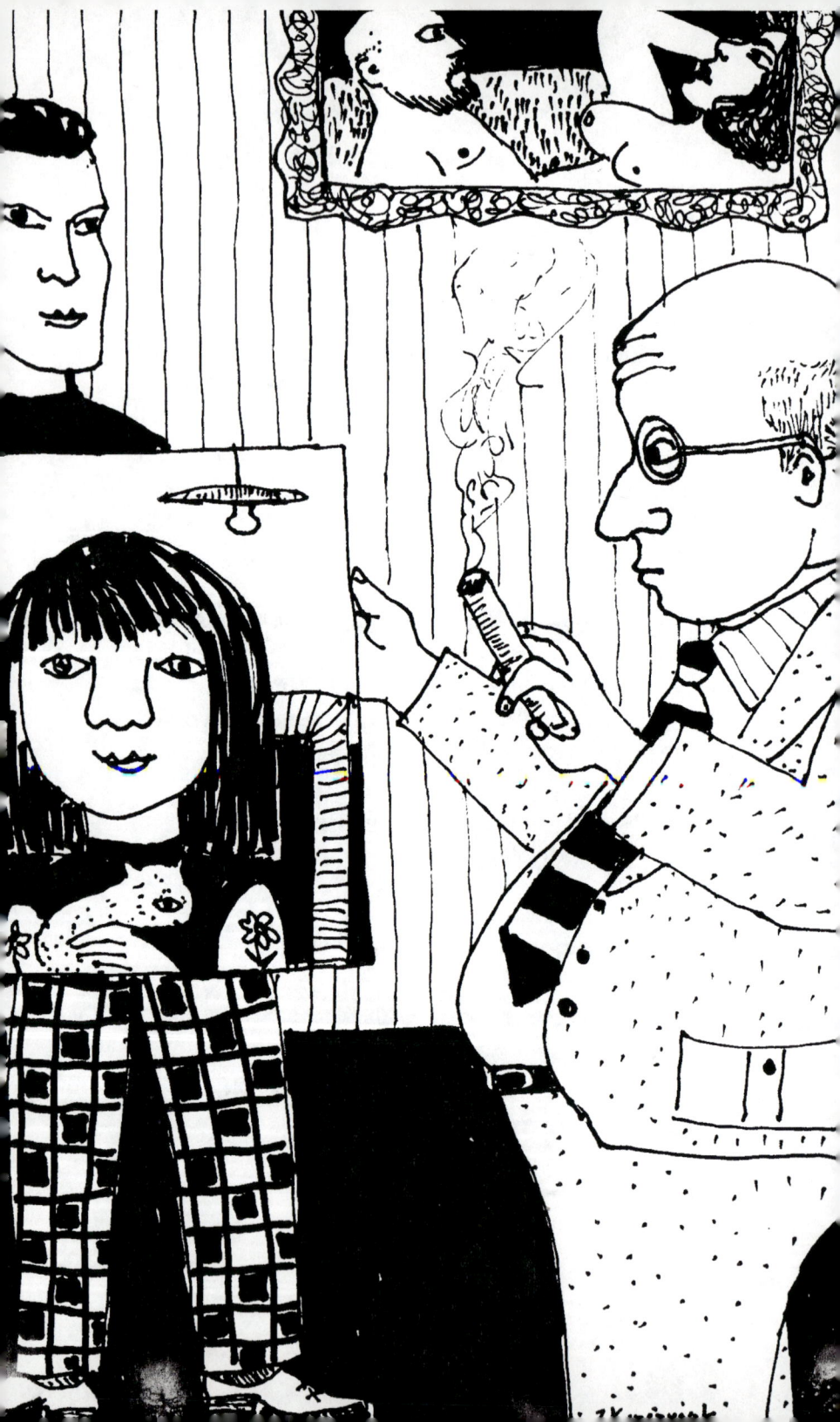

15

Zurich made a huge impression on me: watches, watches, watches everywhere.

Before entering the downtown area, we stopped at a small motel for the night. In the morning, having had a restful sleep and a generous breakfast of ham omelet, orange juice and fresh toast, we washed the car and changed our shirts. Clean and freshly shaved, with our shoes polished to perfection, we cruised down the main drag of Zurich, keeping our eyes open for galleries. On Banhoffstrasse I spotted a huge display window containing paintings in richly gilded frames.

"We'll try here," I told Zbyszek. While he parked the car, I stepped into the gallery, where I was greeted by the yellow eyes of a cat sitting on the desk, its tail twitching nervously. A skinny woman with brightly painted lips was petting the cat.

"How can I be of service?" she asked.

"I am a painter on my way to Paris . . . "

"Just a moment," she said, picking up the receiver.

"Herr Neupert?"

She spoke on the phone for several minutes. Soon a

small man in a grey suit came down the stairs. Staring through golden frames, Herr Neupert's eyes examined me from head to toe. When he had finished, I showed him my portfolio, which contained photos of the paintings I had in the car. Neupert looked at them with interest.

"Where are these paintings?" he asked. "Did you bring them with you?"

I nodded my head and pointed at the car.

"I must see them," he said.

Back at the car, I said to Zbyszek, "The fish has taken the bait."

Inside the gallery again, I introduced Zbyszek to Herr Neupert. To my surprise, my travelling companion spoke German quite well and was soon on good terms with our prospective buyer. After Neupert offered us some cigars, I spread out my work on the floor.

"For the most part," said Neupert, "I do not make transactions with artists from beyond the Iron Curtain. Here in Switzerland we don't like Communist art, but this is entirely different."

He chose five of the best canvasses and asked, "How much should I pay for these?"

Sitting on a comfortable sofa, with a cigar in my mouth, I felt like a king. This wealthy gallery in the centre of Zurich was interested in my paintings, and my travelling companion was astonished.

"How much should I pay for these five paintings?" Neupert repeated.

"How much," I asked him, "did you pay for the painting standing on that antique easel?" The painting in question was a still life with a bouquet of blue flowers painted in bold, eclectic strokes.

"That's by Hans Schweiggel, a well-known Swiss painter.

He had a show in Paris. His paintings in that format sell for anywhere from five to seven thousand Swiss francs."

"I want the same."

"What?!" The gallery owner looked as if the ceiling had just collapsed on his head. "Son, how can you compare yourself to Schweiggel? Hans is famous!"

"Famous?" I responded. "And he sells for only five thousand? Anyway, my work is better. This guy Schweiggel imitates Matisse."

Neupert looked at me carefully, as if he were sizing up an opponent. Finally he chose the best canvas, "Malgosia on a Pony," put it aside and offered to pay four thousand francs. "My last offer!" he assured me.

"Done," I said.

I had never seen such money. I folded the four huge bank notes carefully and put them in my pocket. Then I gathered up the rest of my work and rolled it up.

"Give me your address," said Neupert.

I wrote down the Paris address of my Uncle Gienek, my mother's brother, with whom I was planning to stay. After he shook my hand, Neupert slipped a few cigars into my pocket. Zbyszek and I walked out of the gallery, smiling and satisfied. The yellow eyes of the cat followed us out the door.

"Tomorrow is already Easter," Zbyszek pointed out. "Maybe we deserve to stay one day in Zurich. You're a millionaire now. You can afford one night in a good hotel."

And so it happened that my first Easter abroad was spent with Zbyszek Siemaszko in Zurich. My friend photographed the local architectual monuments for the magazine Stolica while I visited the local shops. I sent a beautiful card to my mother and Malgosia.

16

We arrived in Paris at noon a few days later. Zbyszek expertly swerved through the traffic and found Place de Clichy without any problems. It was there that Uncle Gienek lived in an old apartment block. A French woman, middle-aged, with rollers in her hair, opened the door for us.

"Does Gienek Zając live here?" I asked in Polish. My uncle, whom I had not seen for about thirty years, must have heard my voice, because in the doorway he quickly appeared with a smile on his face.

"Is that you, Zbyszek? Adzia wrote me that you had received a scholarship to come to Paris. Welcome," he said, giving me a warm hug. Then he stepped back to take a good look at me.

"You are the spitting image of Ignac," he concluded. "Your father and I were good friends. He even painted a portrait of Pilsudzki for me."

"Uncle," I interrupted, "I have a friend waiting downstairs. I must say goodbye to him."

"Why don't you invite him upstairs? Maybe he wants to have a drink."

"Do you want to come upstairs?" I asked Zbyszek once I'd reached his car.

He looked up at the window where my uncle and his companion were standing, and he waved.

"Maybe some other time. I'll have a look for some cheap hotel near the Place Pigalle, not far from here."

"I've heard that's where you find the best whores in the city," I remarked.

Zbyszek smiled. "I'll see you," he said. He started his engine, inclined his head gracefully, and drove off. I never saw him again.

My uncle was very glad that I had come. Emily, his partner, did not understand Polish, so my uncle told her about my father in French.

"This young fellow," he said, nodding at me, "inherited his talent from his father. Zbyszek, aren't you hungry?"

"Yes, I am," I said. "We've been driving for seven hours on an empty stomach."

"Emily, make him some scrambled eggs," said my uncle.

Looking at him as I ate, I realized that he had changed a lot over the years. Once he had been handsome, similar in looks to my grandfather, the only difference being that Grandfather had been taller. But time had not treated him kindly. He now had the eyes of a rodent, shoulders that sloped like a bottleneck, and very poorly made false teeth. The teeth, I discovered, bothered him, so he often left them on top of the television set. Emily, however, pleased him greatly. When she was not selling hats on Place de Clein Court, she cared for my uncle faithfully, although they were not legally married.

My uncle stood in my bedroom as I unpacked my small suitcase.

"What's inside that round canister?" he asked.

"A thirty-five millimetre film about my paintings shot by the Documentary Film Centre in Poland."

My uncle seemed astonished. "Oh, then you must be really good," he said. "They don't make such films for just anyone. . . . Even Ignac never had anything like that . . ."

"In his day they didn't film artists," I said. "Besides, he wasn't really a painter. He toiled from morning to night, but he never produced anything anyone wanted to buy."

My uncle shrugged. "I myself liked Ignac's painting. I mean that "Pilsudski" he whipped up was as real as the living man! 'I'll give you twenty zloty for that painting,' I said to your father once. Forget it! The man thought he was I don't know who. 'I'd rather burn it than sell it for a such a pittance!' he said, slamming the door as he left the house. Mad as a bull, he was. He didn't speak to me for two months. Half a year later, your mother bought the painting for me. It cost me thirty zloty."

My uncle smiled. "The painting is still hanging in our bedroom. Even Emily loves that canvas." He then took me to his bedroom, where I saw the "Pilsudski" hanging next to another painting, a gloomy landscape portraying autumn, and a cheap relief sculpture from Zakopane. The colours in my father's painting had faded, but the varnish seemed as good as new.

"It's as shiny as a monkey's ass," I said to my uncle.

That night I dreamed of my father. This time he neither played violin nor painted. He stood by a sink, peeling potatoes, with a fly sitting on his cheek.

17

I adjusted to life in Paris very quickly. During the first week I went on daily excursions with my uncle to the local market, where Aunt Emily sold hats. Returning home, we would always pass the long Rue de Clichy, where the fish and seafood stands made me hold my nose.

One day my uncle bought me a French text from a bookstall there. Each morning after that, I would cram a dozen new words into my head. "Having no language is like having no head," my uncle was fond of saying. It was curious, though, how, having lived in the city for thirty years, he still spoke a bastardized French. For example, instead of saying, *"Je me suis promene,"* he would say simply, *"Mo promenad."*

After my first week of excursions with my uncle, I began to go out on my own, delving ever further into the labyrinth of Parisian streets. One day I landed on the Place Pigalle, a seedy district with pimps and hookers hanging around. Not far away stood Montmartre with its enormous white cathedral, Sacre Coeur, and a square where local "artistes" turned out an endless series of Parisian scenes for the consumption of visiting American tourists. In those days the swarms of tourists visiting Paris could easily have some proper fun—eating fine food and tasting the services of well-trained "ladies." In the sixties, Paris was a Mecca for artists; there were no less than two hundred thousand painters there, four hundred of which at the most were genuinely good ones. Of course, I counted myself among the latter, though at the time no one knew me—apart from my uncle, my aunt, and the two parrots that lived in the cage that hung from their kitchen ceiling.

Most of the first month of my stay in Paris was spent at Montmartre, which was within easy walking distance of Place de Clichy. One day I wanted to go a little further, so I decided to board the metro for Faubourg St. Honoré. There I discovered a legion of galleries, one of which—Gallerie David Druot—was especially attractive. In the window hung a large canvas in browns and blacks. It was painted with sweeping strokes and simplified forms. There was a king with a golden crown, an oval face, a dot instead of a nose, and a mouth represented by two green lines. He was laughing.

I stood in front of the painting transfixed. The image had an indescribable depth. In the right corner, I noted a modest signature: Clavé. Something in the canvas seemed very familiar; the style was similar to mine. Clavé had used different colours, but the expression of his brush was the same.

After that I passed by a dozen other galleries, but saw nothing else that appealed to me like the Clavé, the image of which remained in my mind's eye as I rode the metro home.

The following Saturday I turned up at David Druot's with my portfolio. The owner, freckled and blond, wore a flower in his boutonnière. When he smiled, I noticed a lot of gold teeth. He looked through my paintings with concentration.

"Pas mal. Pas mal," he murmured through his nose, then wrote something on a piece of paper. "I know a gallery that will be interested in your works," he said. "Gallerie Blue, St. Germaine de Presse."

After a metro ride to the Latin Quarter, I found the gallery. To my great surprise, they were exhibiting Hundertwasser. There, on the black walls of the Paris gallery, hung the same colourful spirals that I had seen in Vienna. The proprietor, a woman in her forties, was soon examining my work.

"How long have you been in Paris?" she asked.

"Five weeks," I answered.

"When you have been here for two years, then we'll talk. We have a lot of talented people here, but talent isn't everything. In Paris work counts, honest, hard work."

Undaunted, I visited several other galleries before finding one run by a Belgian. He looked at only one of my works, "Malgosia with Flowers."

"I have a friend, an Englishman, who runs a gallery on Rue St. Michel," he said, writing the address on a card. "Perhaps he will be interested."

Rue St. Michel, being on the other side of Paris, was too far away to visit that day, so I went home, tossed the roll of canvasses under my bed, and sat down to a meal of fresh potatoes with sour cream. Uncle Gienek poured me some red wine.

"Instead of getting involved with those gallery-asses," he said, "rest, go to the cinematheque. Or, if you prefer to learn something, we'll take you to the Louvre."

That Sunday my uncle and aunt and I went to the

museum. Never in my life had I seen so many masterpieces collected under one roof. I was astonished to discover that Leonardo da Vinci's "Mona Lisa" had a cool background: a mix of Prussian blue with umber. In the reproductions I had seen in Poland, everything had been in shades of brown. The painting itself, set in a rich golden frame and separated from the viewer by a chain, did not make a huge impression on me; Mona Lisa's smile was not as mysterious as the song by Nat King Cole had claimed. By contrast, a small picture by Pieter Breughel showing a peasant with a wooden leg shook me to my very core.

What a shame, I thought, that this wonderful artist was not discovered until twenty years after his death. And how strange that the delay was probably caused by his fondness for painting peasants. In Breughel's time, a peasant's place was strictly in the fields, tilling the soil. No one would consider hanging a painting of a peasant in a chateau or a castle. By Rembrandt's time, things had changed a little. He could afford to paint plebeians, though he still preferred to paint rich city merchants, old rabbis, and soldiers on horseback.

The refined world of Rembrandt's shadow, out of which emerged the faces of his time, spoke far more to me than did the giant Delacroix canvas "Bastylia," which was full of political undertones. Vincent van Gogh made my heart beat faster. No one has been able to paint in yellow as he did. His "Sunflowers" reached beyond the boundaries of human capabilities. I wondered if he had had to cut off his ear in order to paint like that.

Picasso, in my opinion, shocked more through his original forms adopted from primitive art, than through his use of colour. He admired Matisse because he was unable to compose hues like his friend. When he was starting work on the cubist movement, along with Georges Bracque, the Frenchman surpassed him in the manipulation of colour. As I looked at Picasso's paintings, I remembered the day two years earlier in the Hotel Monopol in Wroclaw, when the waiters had wanted to throw Picasso out because he had taken off his shirt. The intervention of Party officials on Picasso's behalf almost provoked an international incident. Picasso, you see, was a member of the Communist Party in France and was therefore entitled to special treatment in Poland. He had come to Wroclaw for the Peace Congress and the Party was determined to make his stay pleasant. Poor Antos, one of the waiters at the hotel, had not realized this. He landed on the street without a job—and was lucky to have avoided landing in the hole.

Upon returning home after five hours in the Louvre, I took out the roll of canvasses I had been storing under my bed and looked at them for a long time. In the kitchen, leaning against the wall, stood a canvas I had begun a week or so earlier. The subject was Place de Clichy as seen from a window. Furious, I pulled my wet brush along the length of the canvas and destroyed everything I had painted.

"How could you?" my uncle cried.

"This is shit," I said.

I carried the canvas into my room, then I stood at my window and observed the street below. I thought of my little Malgosia whom I had left behind in Poland.

For the next few months, I would paint nothing but my daughter's face. Sadness and nostalgia would direct the brush on my canvas . . . .

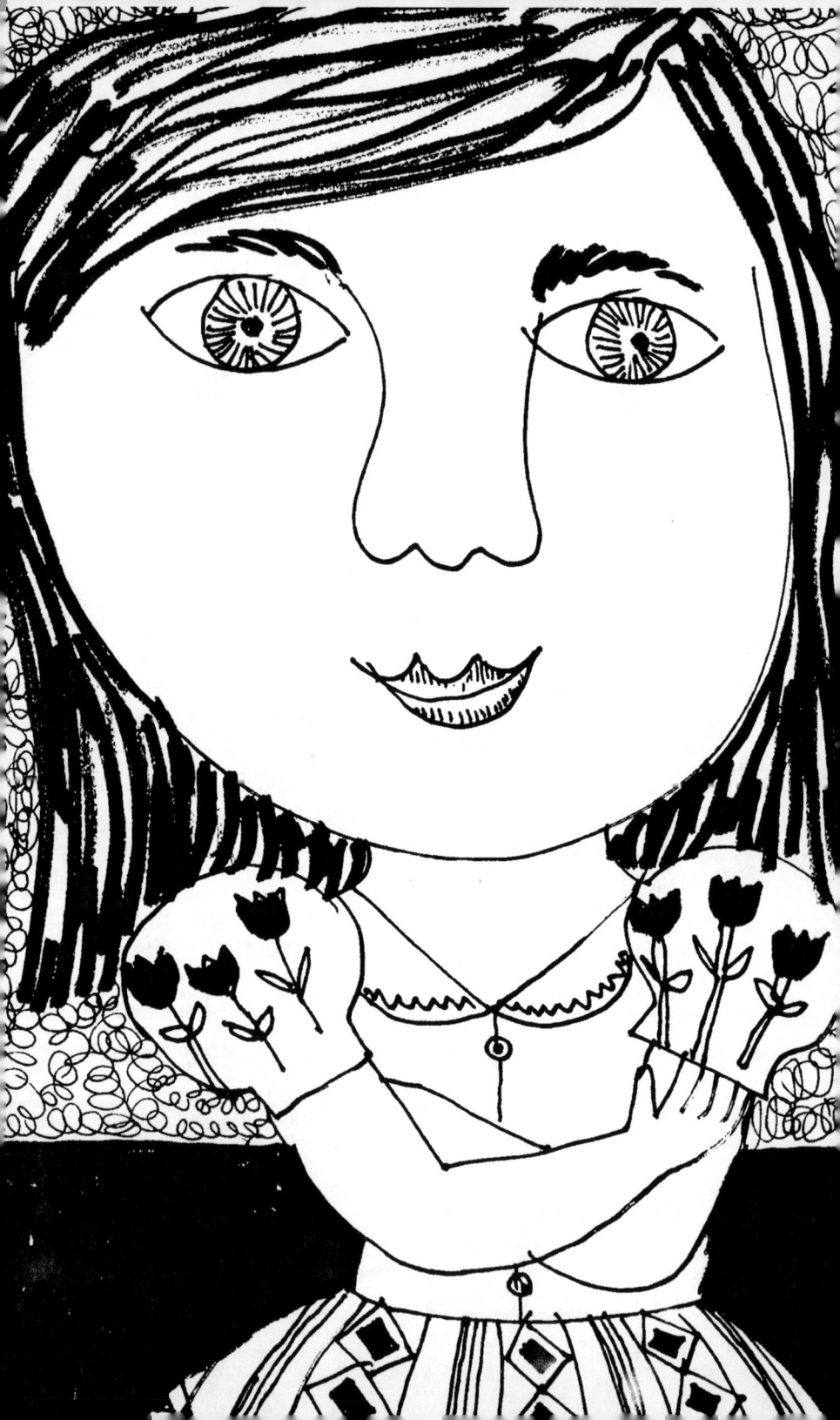

18

The Polish Club on Rue LaJandre was a meeting place for immigrants, refugees, students like myself—anyone feeling lost and lonely in Paris and craving some conversation in their mother tongue.

"Kupczynski, what are you doing here?" came a familiar voice.

At a neighbouring table, right next to the door, sat Zbyszek Cybulski, the actor from Warsaw. I had met him for the first time at the Zacheta State Gallery during a national exhibition. Seemingly inebriated, he had stood on all fours in front of Straszewski's painting and started barking. Then he approached me and said in a completely sober voice, "All of these avant-garde jerks can kiss my ass!" When he asked about my paintings later that evening, I showed him a canvas that was hanging on the opposite side of the gallery beside a large sculpture by Alfonse Karny. Cybulski smiled.

"Interesting, that girl of yours on a horse. I like her green face. You paint from the heart." Then he shook my hand and walked out of Zacheta.

The second time I saw him was in the Literary Club,

where I had my solo debut. I showed twenty-five canvasses, several of them portraits of my little Malgosia. Zbyszek was enchanted. So were Kobiela and Afanysjew, the former a poet, the latter a satirist who wrote for Przekroj. Afanysjew presented me with a bunch of radishes, saying, "I give flowers to my enemies, but to my friends, radishes."

Pleased to see him again, I joined Cybulski for a drink. Like me, he had received a government scholarship worth sixty thousand francs. Unlike me, he was being paid to study acting.

"I've already seen East of Eden seven times," he told me. "What a remarkable person James Dean is. And you, Kupczynski, what's new with you?"

"Nothing but bad luck," I said. "I go from gallery to gallery, like an idiot, but no one wants my paintings. They all say, 'Come back in five years, and then we'll talk.' But in five years I may have cashed in."

We ate pea soup and followed up with some bread.

"Did you bring *The Hues of Joy and Sadness* with you?" he asked, referring to the documentary film financed by a production house on Chelmska Street about three Warsaw painters, the brothers Sliwinski and myself. Zbyszek had seen it several times.

"I must admit I just don't understand those two other guys," he said, "especially the one that painted his own funeral for fifteen years. A skeletal mare, a funeral procession approaching a grave in the green moonlight? Brr. You'd never find that painting above my bed."

"Your paintings," Zbyszek continued, "are happy and colourful. They remind me of childhood."

Then he laughed, exposing a row of unbelievably white, beautiful teeth.

"Why don't you bring this film? We'll show it in the

BBC Club's presentation of short commentaries about Poland. There will be a few journalists from home and a lot of important personalities from the Parisian art scene. Maybe someone will take an interest in your Malgosias."

The next day I took the film to a small hotel on rue St. Michel, where Zbyszek lived. The screening took place on the following Saturday. In the first part of the program, the films featured were about Kazimierz, Nowa Huta, and the rebuilding of Warsaw. Then they showed *The Hues of Joy and Sadness*. When the screening was over, Zbyszek dragged me out onto the stage, where I received a warm round of applause. Sitting in the audience, unbeknownst to me at the time, was André Schoeller, the owner of the famous gallery on rue Miromesuil 23.

One week later, I met Zbyszek at the Polish Club again.

"Thanks to you I have a contract with André Schoeller's gallery," I called out with enthusiasm. "They're giving me a hundred thousand francs for five paintings!"

"Don't thank me," he said. "Thank your own talent."

"If I have such a talent, then why didn't the others want me?"

Zbyszek laughed and said, "In this world talent isn't everything. What counts most are your connections, who recommends you, who knows you. Do you remember the story of the fabulous Spanish pianist Isaac Albéniz? He had more enemies than friends because he was too good. Rejected in Spain, he went to live in Bolivia. A few years later came the news of his untimely death. And Spain, where ten years had passed without a word about Albeniz, went wild, calling him great . . . wonderful . . . unforgettable. In his honour, they organized a music competition offering huge cash prizes to those who could best interpret his compositions. And Albeniz, who was not dead after all, and after whom the competition was named, decided to enter. And guess what? He was weeded out in the preliminaries!" Zbyszek laughed and laughed. "I was also told I had no talent. But you . . . a hundred thousand francs in exchange for five paintings. Not a bad start for a young painter from Poland."

"Not bad?" I asked. "It's fantastic—the best thing that's ever happened to me."

We talked a few more hours away, then said goodbye. I never saw him again. Zbyszek Cybulski, one of Poland's greatest screen actors, died tragically, falling under a train as he tried to jump aboard while drunk. Death took him at an early age, just like his idol James Dean. Every time I see one of his films I have tears in my eyes.

19

Painting for André Schoeller took up a lot of my time. I was determined to give him only the best. I worked long and hard on each and every canvas. At times I would repaint the same picture several times before I was finally satisfied with the results. Once, I fell asleep on the floor of my studio with my brush still in my hand. I dreamt of Malgosia, who was holding a blue flower in her hand. "Daddy," she said, "I brought this for you, so you wouldn't forget about me." I woke up and I gave the child in my painting a blue forget-me-not. Schoeller hung the canvas in his office.

In his gallery, Schoeller had some work by a man called Dalquat, a small, aggressive Frenchman utterly convinced of his own greatness. He painted smooth backdrops, mostly in some shade of brown or red. Then with one stroke of a broad brush, he would make a white irregular line that looked like the kind of mark a dog wagging its tail might make. Another painter, Hartung, worked in a similar manner, although he was more expressive. His sense of colour was also superior.

One day at the end of the month, when I turned up on

rue Miromeznil to get my money, Schoeller paid out my one hundred thousand francs in especially high spirits because he had just sold "Malgosia on a Cow" to a man called Hans Hofman, the owner of a prestigious gallery in Munich.

"How much?" I asked.

"Half a million francs!" he laughed. "Five times the amount I pay you per month. This confirms my hunch, that one can make a lot of money off you."

"I'm glad," I said. "When are you going to start paying me some more?"

"After a show."

Back at home later that day, when I told my uncle how much Schoeller had received for the portrait of Malgosia, he shook his head in disbelief.

Around that time I met an American girl from Texas named Inez at the Café Select. She invited me to her studio under the pretext of showing me her work. After downing two bottles of wine I landed in her soft bed. As it turned out, her father was an executive of the Texaco Company. He was loaded and generous with his daughter, so Inez could spend pretty much whatever she liked. For the next month, she took care of my every need. We painted together and enjoyed the lavish dinners she prepared. By the end of the month though, I'd had enough, so I moved out. I had begun to think a lot about my family in Poland, especially my little Malgosia.

Shortly after leaving Inez, I sat with André Schoeller on the terrace of the Café Select, looking at the traffic on the street. At that time of the day painters gathered there, as did girls in miniskirts and all kinds of musicians. One of these was Alfred, a skinny guy with sunken cheeks and wisps of grey hair escaping from underneath his cheap toupee.

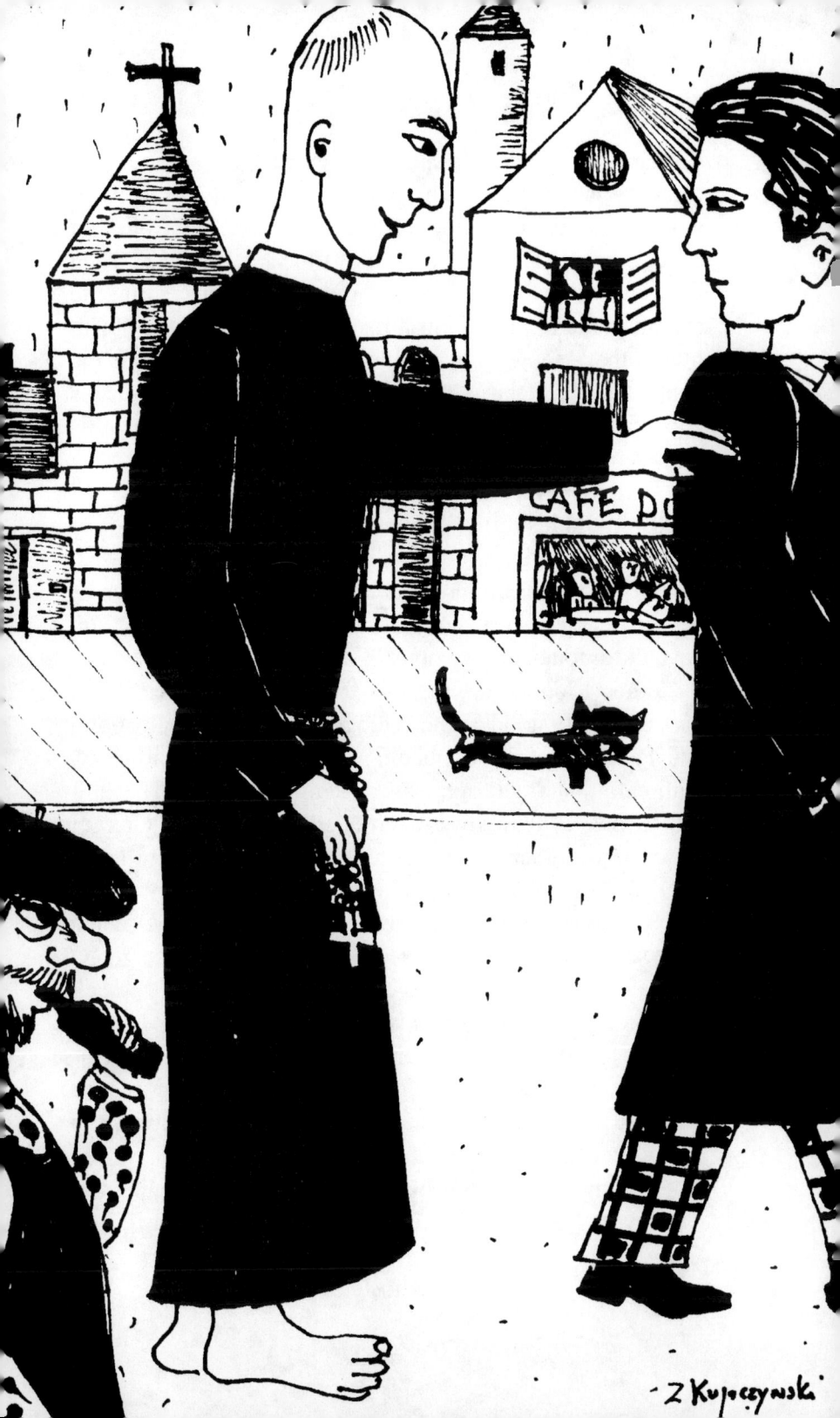

Wearing his trademark tattered tails, each time he entered the café he performed his well-established ritual. After coughing to get our attention, he would take his violin out of its case and announce, "an aria from La Traviata." Then he would draw his bow across the strings, tormenting the old instrument, producing all sounds possible (along with others that seemed impossible). Incapable of playing the simplest tune, he was the unparalleled master of squeaks and groans. Yet people laughed and threw coins into his violin case, amused by his inability to play.

"In Paris, every artist can find a patron," André observed as Alfred did his thing.

After André left, I began sketching a girl selling flowers. Just as her slender figure was taking shape on my piece of paper, someone placed an arm on my shoulder and said, "You haven't forgotten how to draw?" The voice was familiar.

When I looked up, there in front of me, dressed in his dark cassock, stood Father Gongol, Doctor of Philosophy and Theology at the Capuchin Monastery. Tall as a ladder, with ears that stuck out, he was smiling like the Cheshire Cat, exposing two rows of crooked teeth. Father Gongol was, among other things, an art collector. In Poland I had sold him several of my paintings.

"What are you doing here?" he asked. "Did you also get a scholarship?"

Since I was too busy staring at his familiar dark cassock and rosary to answer quickly, he sat down before I could respond and ordered a pitcher of red wine. I noticed immediately that he still smelled of garlic. He had come to Paris, he said, because he had had enough of the Capuchin monastery and wanted to see the world.

Thinking of nothing else to say, I asked, "Remember when you tried to seduce Halina Knapik, the pillar of

Polish sculpture?"

"Yes, of course," he laughed as he poured himself a glass of wine. "And I would have succeeded if not for that bell rope in the chapel."

"In Warsaw you had the reputation of being a wild monk who was never without plans for some mischief."

"A world without pranks is like a landscape without water," he said, slapping my back. "You big lug, it's good to see you! You'll make a career for yourself here. I know it."

"I already have," I laughed. Then I told him about my contract with Schoeller.

"I've heard of Schoeller's gallery. His father built up the business."

"How do you know?" I asked, regarding the monk with surprise.

Listening to his answer now, I remembered the first time I had met him. I was working at the time on a painting called "Monte Cassino," which was full of red poppies. Nothing was working out. I was mad at the whole world. Just as I was about to touch up the painting with some green, someone knocked and opened my door

"Son! Leave that painting alone," cried out a man I'd never seen before, who was standing there with my friend Jas Fajdak. "It's sold!"

"To whom?" I asked.

"To me, of course," he replied. After paying me a good price on the spot, he invited Fajdak and me to accompany him to his monastery.

His small room, which had a little window facing Gold Street, was black with smoke. Cigarette butts were strewn all over the floor. Our discussion centred on art, what it is and why one cannot live without it. Fajdak, who was an electrician by trade (though he too collected paintings), did not agree with Father Gongol's theory.

"My grandfather hasn't got one painting on all his walls and he enjoys life just fine."

"Your grandfather is a moron," Gongol retorted, then turned to me.

"Think of it! Nothing on his walls! Not even a Virgin Mary. I'd go crazy . . ."

Just then someone knocked on the door, and a small plump monk resembling a buttered doughnut entered the cell.

"I beg your pardon, Father," he spoke meekly. "Father Gerwazy wanted to have his confession. He . . ."

"You tell Father Gerwazy he can kiss my ass. He should stop sticking his nose in the wrong places, then he wouldn't have to go to confession every second day." Then, having disposed of Father Gerwazy, Father Gongol threw his burning cigarette on the floor and extinguished it with his bare foot.

Sitting with him now on the terrace of the Café Select in Paris, listening to him explain how he had come to know about André Schoeller, I hoped he hadn't changed.

20

Several days after my meeting with Father Gongol, I made my way to the Polish Consulate to extend my passport for another six months. A few other people were sitting in the waiting area while I filled out the forms and handed them to the secretary at the wicket.

"This won't take long," she told me. After waiting for about twenty minutes, I was summoned into an office where I saw a man with the face of a gorilla sitting at a desk. He had my papers in his hand.

"Kupczynski, is it?"

His rough tone put me on my guard. When you're addressing a gorilla, I thought to myself, you have to stay on top of the conversation. The specimen behind the desk regarded me coldly. He did not like the fact that I wanted to stay longer in France.

"It's time you went back to Poland. You're needed for work there."

"What kind of work? I'm an artist, a painter. I don't work, I create!"

The gorilla looked at me as if I had just dropped from another planet. "I'm not interested in what it is that you do," he said. "There'll be no extensions. It's time for you to pack your bags and head home."

I was furious, and was warning him that he had better listen to my request when another man entered the room. He had an intelligent face and was well dressed. A smile spread across his attractive face.

"What is going on in here?" he asked in a baritone voice.

The gorilla informed him that I did not want to return to my native Poland.

"I paint for André Schoeller's gallery," I told the newcomer. "He's organizing a show for me. Won't that be good publicity for our nation? A Polish artist exhibiting in the French capital?"

"I agree with you, Zbigniew," said the man in the suit, who turned out to be the consul. "It's a grand thing to possess a talent. We'll extend your passport for another six months. For artists, Paris is the same as water for fish."

He took my passport from the gorilla's paw and sealed it with a large stamp. After saying thanks, I promised him an invitation to the opening of my show, which I thought was a sure thing. But, as they say, even when a man fires a pistol, God still guides the bullet. Everything unfolded in a way I did not expect.

21

A week or so after my visit to the Polish Consulate, André and I descended the stairs leading to a dry basement, where he stored various artists' work. He had seven under contract. Two of these had already been launched, a Spaniard by the name of Maliarez and the Frenchman from Marseilles, Pier Talquat. André sold their work at high prices, which allowed him to invest in new talent.

"I'll show you a very interesting Turk by the name of Abdin," he said. "His work is quite engaging."

"More so than mine?" I asked.

"Different," said André, smiling. "He is Turkish, and you are Polish. You can't compare apples and oranges."

I began examining the work. The Turk used a lot of yellow. He paired with black, white and Prussian blue. The painting had no subject as such; it was completely abstract —only stains and lines applied with sweeping brushstrokes. Everything radiated with life tinged with a note of nostalgia.

"He's been working for me for close to three years now," said André. "Next year I will organize a show for him. I'll invest some money in publicity and he'll take off, just like Dalquat, who sells for anywhere from half a million to three million francs per canvas. Art is not a bad business . . . when you know who to promote."

"I like Clavé," I commented. "It would be nice to meet him some day. "

André started laughing. "Nothing would come of it if you did. He's an arrogant bastard who imitates Picasso."

"Perhaps," I said, "but his way of doing it is very interesting."

Schoeller shrugged. "I prefer your work. It has a child's naïveté and something which forces people to think."

"Then when are you going to organize a show for me?"

"You don't have enough paintings. It hasn't even been one year since you came here. Abdin has been waiting three."

"I'm not able to wait so long."

"But I am. I have loads of time. And you, each month you get sufficient pay to be able to enjoy yourself as an artist in this city. Do you know how many painters there are in Paris who are perishing from hunger? They would give a lot to be in your shoes."

When we emerged from the basement into the gallery, André pointed to a huge canvas hanging by the window. "Take Gutrie, for example, who had to go through a healthy amount of hard work before he became what he is now."

"His painting resembles dirty clouds pouring down rain," I said.

"Rain that smells of money. Do you know how much a Gutrie sells for? Ten million!"

"If I painted like that I think I'd slit my throat."

"You don't have to," André laughed. "Paint as you have always painted and be patient. If you listen to me, you'll go far."

"Yes," I said, "but are you willing to consider paying me more for my paintings now?"

"Out of the question," André responded, adding some more cognac to my glass.

22

I left the gallery with mixed feelings. On the one hand, I was flattered that André preferred my paintings to Clavé's, but on the other, I was angry for having to wait so long for my own show. The metro station was around the corner, so I rode to the Polish Club to have dinner. Their menu was decent and one was bound to meet someone interesting there. This time, I encountered Zdzic Majchrzak, a graduate of the Academy of Fine Arts in Warsaw. Having left his wife and children at home, he had applied for political asylum in France. He was sitting with Marek Hlasko, a writer who was also a truck driver.

I never particularly liked Marek, whose novels reminded me of Hemingway. We had met for the first time in the office of the newspaper PO PROSTU (SIMPLY) where, from time to time, I did illustrations. On one occasion, I watched from the window of the editorial office while he, dead drunk, ran in through the gates, knocking over a child on a sled. Back in Poland, Hlasko had befriended Irek Irendinski, who had written a play entitled "The Third Breast." The foundation of their friendship was vodka. In time Jas Himilsbach joined them. Although he was more talented than Irendinski and more humane than Hlasko, he too had abandoned the world for alcohol.

When I sat down at Hlasko's table, he winked at me with a blood-shot eye. Trying to be funny, he asked if I was still painting children.

"Yes," I answered, "since that is the happiest time in anyone's life."

"Not in mine!" Hlasko guffawed loudly. "That was the only time I was not allowed to have vodka."

A few days later I ran into André Schoeller again. He was angry because of my request for a raise.

"I have enough of these children," he said, referring to my portraits od Malgosia. "Why don't you get on with something new, some nudes or a still life?"

"If you don't like them, someone else will buy my stuff," I told him.

"I was only joking," he said quickly. "Paint what you like."

I left the gallery without a word of goodbye and took the metro to Montparnasse. At the Café Select I met a girl from Tunis who had deep black eyes and the lithe lines of a cat. We went to the cinema. She put her hand on my knee. I can't remember the movie, but I know that afterwards I landed in her flat on St. Michel. I'll never forget that night. She had skin like satin. The next day I began painting her. When I finished I was exhausted, as if I had just trekked across the desert. On shaky legs, with the canvas under my arm, I dragged myself to the metro. André was delighted. He hung the nude over his desk in place of the Futrie.

"You must have toiled over this one," he remarked with a note of jealousy in his voice, looking at my pale face. "I'd love to meet this lady."

23

Before leaving Paris I ran into Father Gongol again at the Polish Club. The place had become his home. He was sitting with Jan Lebenstein, a painter from Warsaw. We did not like each other. Lebenstein was a talented artist, but a terribly envious one. He had chosen to visit my show in Cepelia (a line of stores selling Polish art and craftwork) at midnight to prevent anyone catching him admiring the work of Kupczynski. I know because I was walking home from a nightclub at the time and saw him there.

"What are you doing here at this time?" I had asked him, but he left without a word.

On this occasion, when he noticed me approaching Father Gongol and him, he quickly said goodbye to Gongol and left again.

"What have you done to him?" the monk inquired.

"I have painted better than he has."

"You have painted differently. You paint children."

"And he . . . rats humping!" I retorted.

"But Lebenstein did get a show at the Museum of Modern Art," Gongol pointed out.

"Politics, politics, politics," I said.

"I agree with you there," said Gongol with a laugh, "although you must admit he has talent."

A couple of months later I was on my way to deliver some more paintings to André Schoeller's gallery. It was chilly and the leaves were starting to fall. The gallery, it turned out, was closed. A card hung in the window: "I've gone to St. Tropez. Back on Oct. 10th." I walked into the nearby gallery of Paul Ginz, a friend of André's.

"He didn't leave any money for me?" I asked.

The Frenchman shook his head. He started to leaf through my paintings.

"Why don't you sell these ones to me? I can pay well."

Furious with André, I began to bargain. The Frenchman was ready to buy my paintings alright, but he didn't want to pay a decent price. For my part, I was in no mood to give in. After a while we settled on half a million francs for six paintings—five times the amount I had been getting from Schoeller.

"Tell André that he can kiss my ass," I said, putting my money in my pocket. Tomorrow, I'm leaving for Poland."

Later that evening, my uncle expressed his satisfaction with my decision to go back home. "You can paint anywhere," he told me. "And your mother will be happy to see you back."

The next day I bought my train ticket and some presents for Malgosia and my mother. The day after that, at 8:30 a.m., I boarded a train bound for Poland. Twenty hours later I stepped onto the platform of the Warsaw train station.

24

As I walked home, I discovered that Warsaw had not changed at all. The people were still eyeing each other with suspicion, feuding while they stood in line for a taxi, and assaulting one another with the stink of their bodies. The citizens of the capital city of the Polish Republic had yet to discover the charm of a little thing called deodorant.

At home, I was greeted by my mother. Malgosia, who had grown enormously in the past year, threw herself in my arms. I kissed her round cheeks. Holding her tight, I felt blissfully happy. After letting her go, I gave the gifts I had brought from Paris: a wool sweater for my mother and for my daughter a big doll whose eyes blinked when she was cradled.

"You've gotten so skinny in Paris," my mother remarked.

"I was painting; I had no time to eat."

"I'll bet you were constantly bar hopping. You need to settle down. Otherwise, with your way of life, you'll catch some sort of venereal disease."

"Do we really have nothing else to talk about?" I said. "I just got here."

"All right, all right," mother said. "I'll go heat up some of the potato pancakes left over from lunch."

That evening, exhausted from my journey, I crawled into bed and immediately fell into a deep sleep. In the morning, I woke up to the smell of fresh coffee. When I entered the kitchen, I saw mother combing Malgosia's long hair.

"Daddy, will you be painting me again?"

"Of course! You are my best model. One gallery in Paris has close to sixty of your portraits!"

I started to tell my mother of my successes.

"You should have stayed longer," she said. "Are you crazy? You were earning good money."

"I was missing you too much. Besides, Paris is terribly expensive. I was barely making ends meet. And the late nights were beginning to wear me out."

"There! You see?" said my mother. "You were living the life of a gigolo. Decent people go to bed early, and they go to work early in the morning."

"Daddy is an artist," Malgosia said.

"That's true, my child. Your daddy is an artist," I said as I began to examine the paintings I had done before leaving for Paris.

25

At the Polish Association of Visual Artists on Foksal, I saw some familiar faces. Alfred Lenica was playing checkers with Henia Strazewski, while Roman Opalka and Sbyszek Makowski were looking on. In the line-up for soup, I ran into Borowski, a snobbish art critic who wrote in a pompous, inflated style. "Painters are incapable of logical thought," he would pronounce. "I prefer to discuss art with a chemist or a physicist." I had never been able to read one of his articles to the end. And he, for his part, did not think of my paintings as serious art.

Looking at him standing in the soup line, it was difficult to imagine that he had ever been a child. No wonder he didn't like me or my art. People who have lost all sense of what it means to see through the eyes of a child always deride lightheartedness. This is why Salieri could not stand Mozart, who loved to laugh and play the fool. Yet for all his seriousness, Salieri could not come close to the beautiful music that flowed from Mozart's fingers.

After I returned to Poland, everything started to go wrong. I was refused residence at Kordegarda, a state gallery in the Krakowski Przedmiescie that was designated for individual exhibitions, although I had applied for it before my departure for Paris. I had known even then that there was always a long waiting list. When I sought an explanation at the secretariat of the Polish Association of Visual Artists, Mrs. Wilkomska informed me that my place in the gallery had been given to Antek Glas.

"This year, there have been a lot of changes in the artistic realm. Your paintings are somewhat too modern for Kordegarda. Your forms are becoming increasingly abstract. Take your lips, for example, a horizontal brushstroke or some wavy lines that represent a nose . . ."

"I'm approaching an ever greater synthesis," I said, ready to explode.

"The Party is not terribly impressed by this," responded Wilkomska, looking at her watch. "Mr. Kupczynski, I really must be going to the assembly."

Once this idiotic interview was over, I walked home by way of the Old City, trying not to step on the horseshit that stuck to the cobblestones. In the town square, there stood many carriages with drivers that resembled morticians. Why, I wondered, had I returned to this country?

The following night I made my way to Krokodyl (The Crocodile), a popular nightclub, to dance away my blues. My companion was Azorek, a voluptuous woman with a beautiful, sensual face. We were dancing an Argentinean tango, enjoying every move, when someone pushed me vigorously from behind.

"Watch out!" I warned a huge guy with a camera slung over his shoulder. "You're not the only person on the dance floor."

The next thing I knew, we were at each other's throats, exchanging furious punches. He was awfully strong, and for a time I thought he would get the better of me. But I managed to land one effective punch on his chin that sent him crashing to the floor.

"I give up," he groaned.

I returned to our table, where Azorek was sitting scared. A waiter approached us.

"My compliments," he said. "That goon finally met his match. He thinks that just because he's a reporter for Trybuna Ludu he can do as he pleases."

Azorek was happy and proud of me. She slipped her hand under mine. Later we walked home together through the Old City, her high heels clicking loudly on the cobblestones. I felt like a hero, and my joy would have been complete had it not been for the fact that I had torn my cashmere jacket, which I'd just bought in Paris for close to two thousand francs.

26

Having been denied the opportunity to exhibit my works at the Kordegarda, I decided to stage my own exhibition. The ideal site, I decided, would be the Barbakan, a reconstructed wall in Warsaw that joined the Old City with the New. All I needed now was someone to assist me, preferably a young painter like Waldemar Smola or Janys Naliwajko. I arranged to meet Waldemar at the Barbakan. He showed up early in the morning with ten of his canvasses, some nails, and a hammer. Except for the two of us, there was not a soul to be seen along the Barbakan.

I had already marked out the spots where the paintings were to hang. After I had pointed these out, Smola began to hammer the nails into the brick wall. I hung up my latest works. In painting them, I had mostly used a palette knife. Listening to the music of Miles Davis and John Coltrane, I had laid down restless, vibrant stains that created an interesting play on the polished surface of my canvas. Succulent black lines dominated, but occasionally a zinc white or a cobalt blue made an appearance. Hanging on the Barbakan and lit by the rising sun, these paintings looked spectacular.

When the sun moved overhead and began to burn,

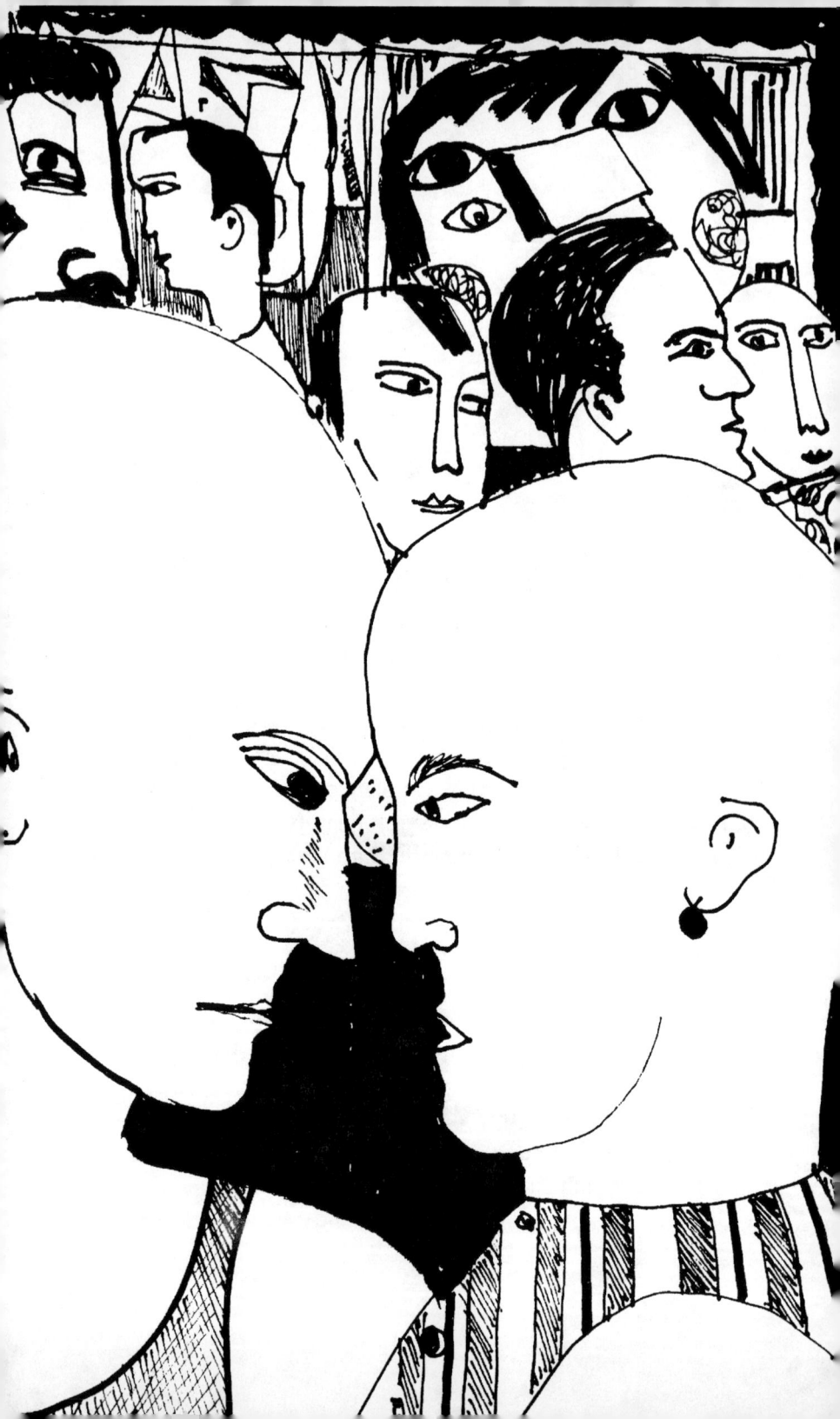

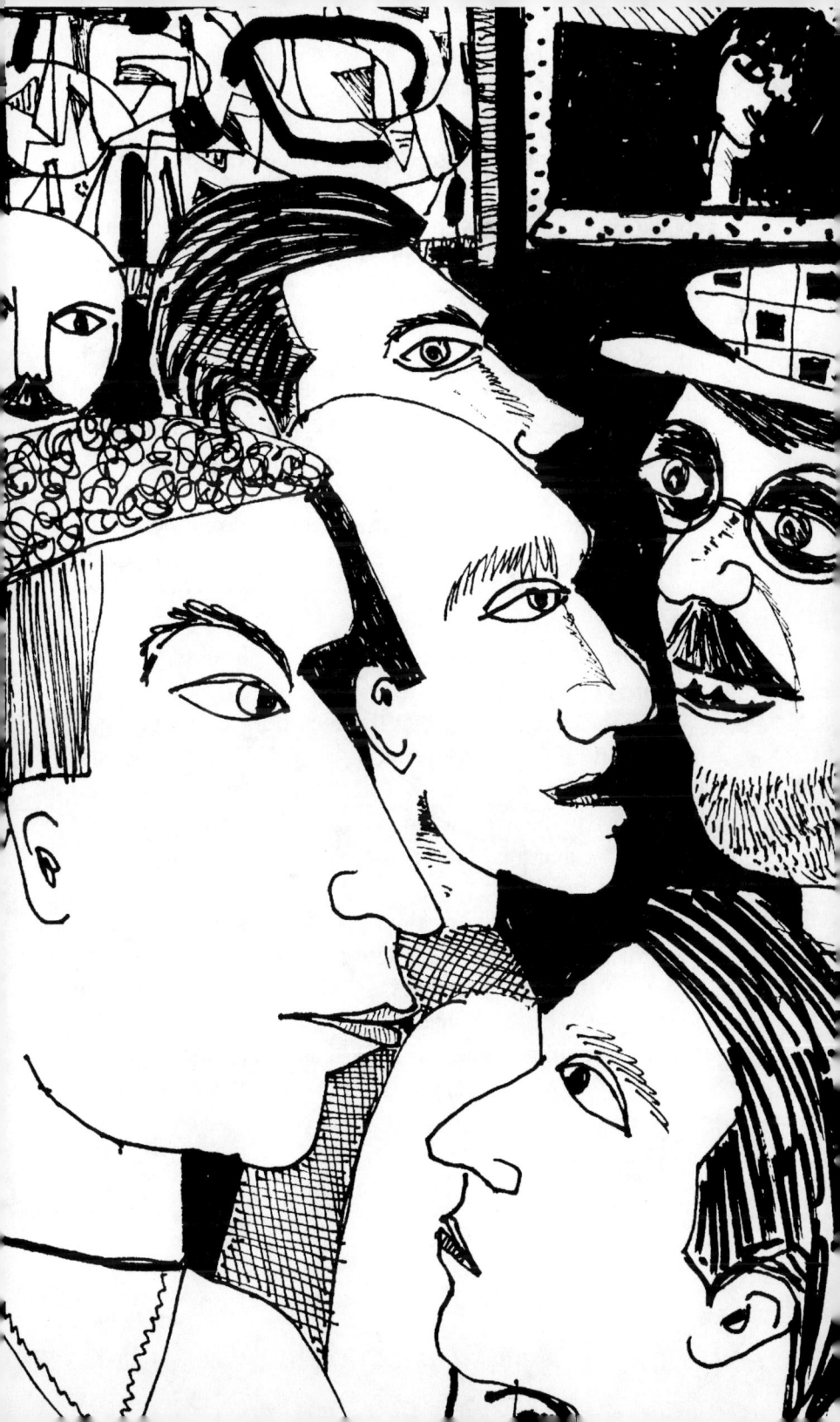

Smola and I relocated to a bench under the shade of an enormous tree and waited for our customers. The first to appear was a mother with two children. Then came a nun in a black habit, two policemen, and a fellow with earphones on.

Over the next two hours about two hundred people turned up, including a number of KGB types with their telltale conspicuous grey suits and smelly feet, a large woman from the magistrate's office, and the chairman of the Warsaw branch of the Polish Association of Visual Artists, Tadeusz Gronowski.

"Zbigniew, what do you think you're doing here?" he asked. "I just had a phone call from the Central Party Commissariat, asking me to find out what in God's name was going on here."

Then, as he looked around at the pictures, a smile appeared on his face.

"There's no denying that these colours knock you out. There will be a bit of commotion around here, but that's a good thing." He lowered his voice. "We've got to show our 'comrades' in the Ministry of Culture that people want something better than that kitsch like 'Pass the Brick Brother' or 'Mother Korea.'"

As I watched his tall figure walk away, I detected the scent of his fine cologne hanging in the air. Then I turned my attention to my canvasses. One, I noticed, needed adjustment. The wind had blown it off balance. Before I could move to straighten it, I heard an unfamiliar voice.

"Are you Mr. Kupczynski?" said a man with two cameras slung over his shoulder.

I nodded.

"May I take your picture?" he said.

"Yes, by all means," I answered.

He immediately began to click away. After taking a few dozen shots, the photographer bought one of my paintings, paying me one hundred U.S. dollars for a small abstract.

"This picture reminds of the field I saw from my window as a kid," he said before shaking my hand and quickly disappearing into the crowd.

When I told Smola of my sale, I learned that he too had sold a painting. His buyer was a Swede from Malmoe who had been happy to pay five hundred coronas for a large abstract. It would not be long, Smola and I agreed, before Maciek (popularly known as "Fat Barrel") turned up to exchange our foreign money for Polish currency.

Later that day, Janys Naliwajko turned up. He had been passing through the Old City by chance and had stumbled upon a crowd of people having a heated discussion about art. Someone had mentioned the Barbakan and he decided to investigate. He was surprised to find Smola and me there.

"You organized a show without me?" he asked us. "What were you thinking of?"

The next morning he showed up with ten of his own canvasses. Each of these, though coloured differently, featured a one-foot-square window cut out of the canvas and then sewn back in place with black or golden thread.

"I have come up with a new style," he bragged, having no idea that dozens of artists before him had done the same thing, including Miliarez and Tapies.

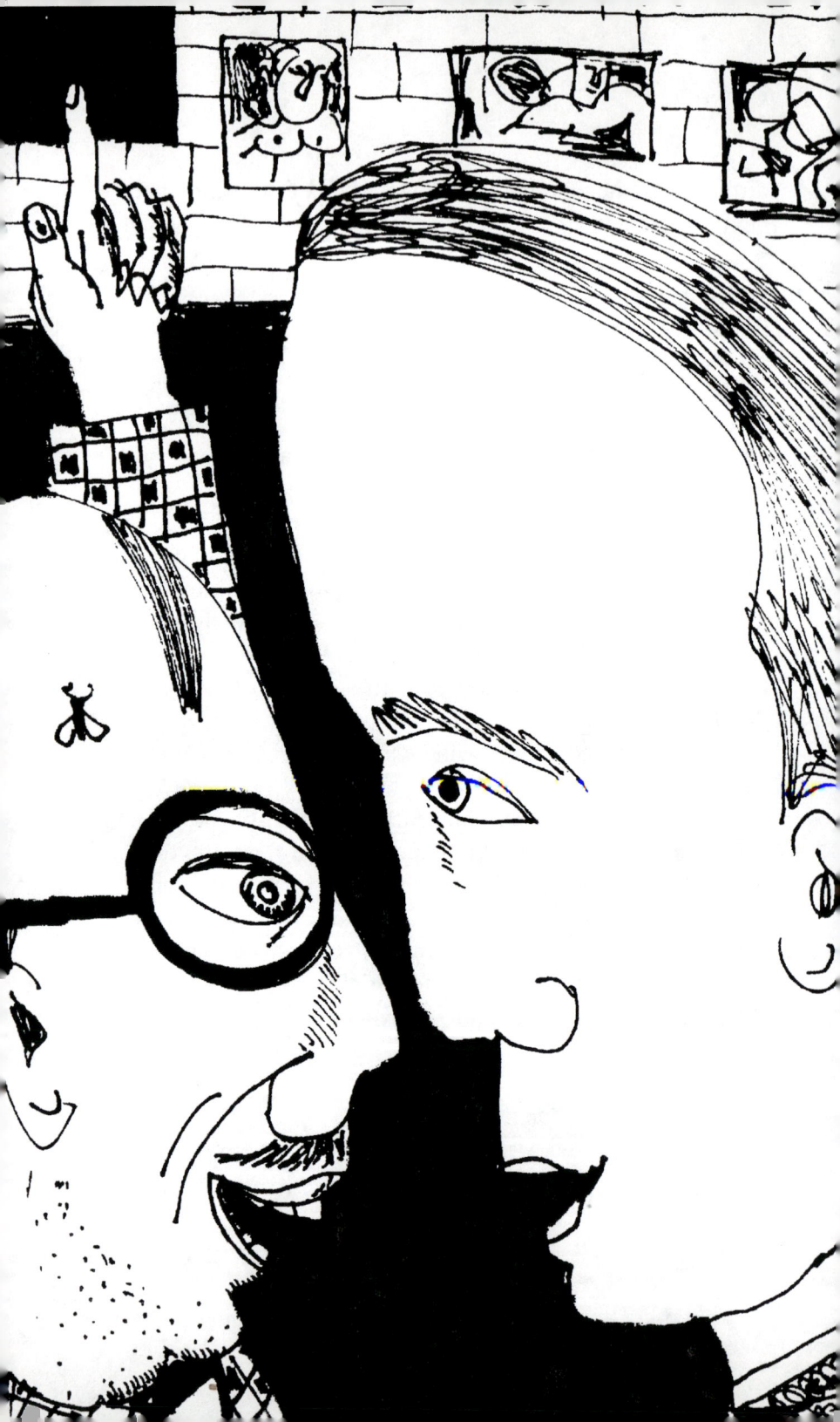

27

In the following months, the exhibit at the Barbakan became a favoured destination for tourists visiting Poland. The party bosses were disturbed by our success and unsure how to respond. Should they close down the show and throw us in the hole, or take advantage of our popularity by observing our visitors? Ordinary citizens were also upset.

"Off to Siberia with them!" shouted a woman in a red cap.

"Kiss maja ass," whispered Janys Naliwajko in her ear. Born in Kiev, he could speak Russian "well enough," as he put it.

Different suspicious types began to hang around the Barbakan. Some played the part of tourists. Some pretended to be painters by hanging up scribbles of their own on the wall. Luckily, we had already taken the prime spots. A fellow we called Mozart, a skinny pike in a felt hat, never abandoned his vigil. He had the typical gaze of a secret policeman—not to mention the giveaway stinking feet. We knew him from an incident that had occurred in the basement of the well-known Polish actor Bronsislaw P., where we stored our paintings. Stone drunk, Mozart had threatened a woman named Zoska with a pistol because, despite his offer of a substantial amount of money, she had refused his request for sex.

Opponents of what we were doing at Barbakan, including comrade Lyzwianski, accused us of conducting a "circus." And in a sense we were. Crowds of people flocked to see the spectacle, and not everything in the show was of good quality. My own work at the time was not always great. Even so, the abstract pieces I churned out sold well—to the constant irritation of my colleagues at the Polish Association of Visual Artists.

One day in August two girls showed up at the Barbakan. They had come to see the artists. I busied myself with the taller of the two, who sat herself down on the bench. Blond with green eyes, she told me that she knew Azorek, with whom I had partied at Krokodyl a few days earlier.

"My name is Elzbieta," she told me. "I'm also a painter."

It was obvious that the girl was interested in me.

"If you like," I said, "I'll show you some more pictures."

After she nodded in agreement, I took her to our basement storage. She had by then caught my drift. Elzbieta's hair, I remember, smelled of autumn. We saw each other for three days. I would have been pleased to go on seeing her, but she decided to bring her paintings to the Barbakan, and she did not have an ounce of talent.

In October, the leaves began to fall from the trees and the weather turned cold. I caught the flu and had to stay home for a couple of days. When I returned, Janis could not contain his excitement. An American actor, he said, with a dimple in his chin—the one who had played the lead in Spartacus—had come to see the show.

"He paid in rubles for one of my pictures. He'd been

visiting family in Russia. His name is Kirk Douglas."

Another celebrity who visited the Barbakan was a slim man with quick eyes by the name of Harold Schonberg. After examining my canvasses for a long time, he sat down on a bench and noted something on his writing pad. Then he walked up to a painting done in browns and reds, ran his hand over its surface, and nodded in approval.

"You must be Mr. Kupczynski."

"How do you know?" I asked.

Ignoring my question, he asked my age, how long I had been painting, where I was born, where I had studied, and whether I had been abroad. I answered these questions patiently while he took notes. Then he got up from the bench to again look at the brown and red picture.

"How much?"

After we agreed on a price he selected another painting, which was a bit smaller, an abstraction in blues. Then he paid in American dollars, shook my hand and told me, "I'm going to write about you in *The New York Times*."

Schonberg's article there, "Old Walls and New Art," spoke (mostly in superlatives) about "a wild boy, Zbigniew Kupczynski, and his gang" who were shaking up the art scene behind the Iron Curtain. Afterwards, articles about the crazy young artists who dared to paint abstraction in defiance of the Communist school of Socialist Realism began to appear regularly in the Western press.

Some weeks after Schonberg's visit, Franco Bertona, the cultural attaché at the Italian Embassy in Warsaw, brought along journalists from the magazine *Europeo* to see the Barbakan show. Some time later a full-page spread of yours truly appeared in the Italian magazine. The caption underneath the photograph read: "Young Rebels." The next page showed Smola holding a palette in his hand. When Smola saw it, he joked, "I must be getting famous."

His words applied to all of us, as my meeting with Gunter Schiller some weeks later at the Bazyliszek Pub made clear. Sitting at a neighbouring table sipping a glass of wine and studying a map of Warsaw, he looked at me from across the aisle and asked, "Do you know where the Bar-ba-kan is? There's supposed to be an art exhibition on the wall."

"Yes," I answered. "You can get my paintings there."

"Really?" His eyes lit up. "What is your name?"

"Kupczynski," I said.

When I took him to the Barbakan, he looked at my paintings for a long time. Eventually he remarked that I must love music.

"Am I right?"

I nodded in agreement. "Without music, our lives would be like a landscape without the sun."

After buying an abstract work in yellow for two hundred dollars, Schiller sat down beside me on a bench. He told me that he was a composer of contemporary music. From his briefcase he took out three records. They had golden covers, each reading "Modern Jazz Quartet." Underneath was his name: "Gunter Schiller, Composer."

"Zbigniew, do you want these records?"

He took a pen out of his pocket and signed the covers: "To my friend, a marvelous painter."

THE NEW YORK TIMES, MONDAY, SEPTEMBER 2, 1962

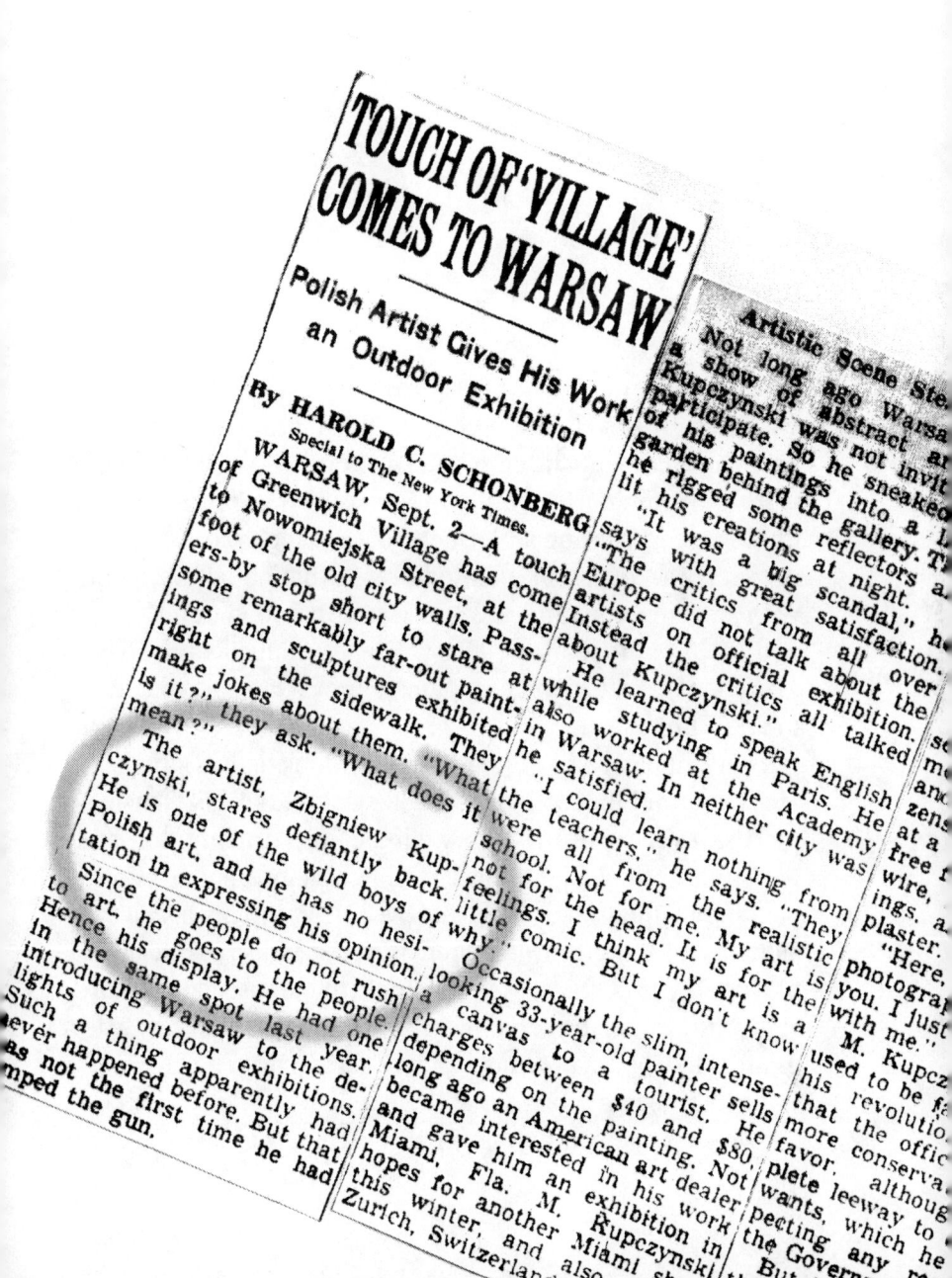

TOUCH OF 'VILLAGE' COMES TO WARSAW

Polish Artist Gives His Work an Outdoor Exhibition

By HAROLD C. SCHONBERG
Special to The New York Times.

WARSAW, Sept. 2 — A touch of Greenwich Village has come to Nowomiejska Street, at the foot of the old city walls. Passers-by stop short to stare at some remarkably far-out paintings and sculptures exhibited right on the sidewalk. They make jokes about them. "What is it?", they ask. "What does it mean?"

The artist, Zbigniew Kupczynski, stares defiantly back. He is one of the wild boys of Polish art, and he has no hesitation in expressing his opinion.

Since the people do not rush to art, he goes to the people. Hence his display. He had one in the same spot last year. Such a thing apparently had never happened before. But that was not the first time he had jumped the gun.

Artistic Scene Ste...

Not long ago Warsa... a show of abstract ar... Kupczynski was not invit... participate. So he sneaked... of his paintings into a l... garden behind the gallery. T... he rigged some reflectors a... lit his creations at night.

"It was a big scandal," h... says with great satisfaction. "The critics from all over Europe did not talk about the artists. Instead the critics all talked about Kupczynski."

He learned to speak English while studying in Paris. He also worked at the Academy in Warsaw. In neither city was he satisfied.

"I could learn nothing from the teachers," he says. "They were all from the realistic school. Not for me. My art is not for the head. It is for the feelings. I think my art is a little comic. But I don't know."

Occasionally the slim, intense-looking 33-year-old painter sells a canvas to a tourist. He charges between $40 and $80, depending on the painting. Not long ago an American art dealer became interested in his work and gave him an exhibition in Miami, Fla. M. Kupczynski hopes for another Miami show this winter, and also one in Zurich, Switzerland.

"Here,... an... zens... free f... wire,... ings, a... plaster.

"Here,... photogra... you. I just with me."

M. Kupcz... used to be fa... his revolutio... that the offic... more conserva... favor, althoug... plete leeway to wants, which he pecting any rece the Government. But he is not w... the future. "The offic... know t... czy..."

28

When we first opened the Barbakan show, Wicek Sliwinski was in his fifties. In the preceding thirty years he had managed to paint only four pictures. Granted, these pictures were intriguing. His "Funeral" showed a rake of a mare pulling a cart bearing a black coffin up a snow-covered hill. A thin crescent moon, painted blue, illuminated the scene with an eerie green light. Wicio was very proud of his work and of his ability as an artist. He introduced himself to everyone he met as the best painter in Warsaw, maybe even in all of Poland.

Unfortunately, he did not want to exhibit at the Barbakan. He was afraid that someone might steal one of his "masterpieces." Yet he came every single day, mainly for the opportunity to engage others in conversations about proper painting methods and (a subject even dearer to his heart) the stupidity of the governing council of the Polish Association of Visual Artists. Wicio was a member of the association himself, but he hated everyone on the governing council. He referred to Chairman Gronowski as "a lefty by convenience." Cybis, a fine arts professor at the Academy of Arts, received far worse judgements. As for Party members at large, Wicio referred to them as "stinking vermin" or "fucking reptiles." No one was safe from this skinny man, whose nose was the colour of a tomato.

He took special pleasure in teasing Janys Naliwajko about his habit of trading paintings for clothing. "Exactly how," he would ask ironically, "has the painter acquired his fine American jacket and his beautiful straw hat?" The jacket and hat in question had been obtained from an America tourist who had been willing to give them, along with forty dollars, in exchange for one of Janys's paintings, a canvas sewn together with black thread. Janys had hoped to obtain the tourist's cowboy shirt in the bargain, but the tourist had refused, saying he wasn't about to walk the streets of Warsaw without a shirt.

Janys's bargaining skills benefited everyone who exhibited at the Barbakan, since he acquired far more clothing than he could use himself. We all walked around in foreign clothing and smoked fine cigars. In keeping with my view of myself as the only ambassador of "serious art," I chose to dress in the Parisian fashion.

One day, Zygmunt Grzybowski, the director of the Cepelia at the MDM (Marszalkowska Residence District) turned up at the Barbakan.

"Mr. Kupczynski? I saw both you and your little daughter in a documentary."

He looked at the canvasses hung all over the brick walls and smiled.

"Why don't you give a couple of your paintings to our store? A lot of tourists visit us: Americans, Germans, Swedes."

We spoke for half an hour and I took a liking to the man. We parted with my promise to paint a special picture for Cepelia. Two days later, I delivered a square canvas to the MDM featuring a white line cutting through a blue-black background. In the upper right hand corner I had pasted a mirror. The title was "The Way to Heaven," the price ten thousand zloty. By the next day all of Warsaw was talking about the painting, and the day after that it disappeared from the store.

"A gentleman with a long nose and slightly wavy hair, who was passing through Warsaw, walked into Cepelia and paid ten thousand zloty for your painting," Grzybowski informed me. The man in question, I later discovered, was Richard Nixon.

The press was soon all over the story: "KUPCZYNSKI SELLS PAINTING TO NIXON." Shortly afterwards, I received a telephone call from the American Embassy. The Consul General John Cabot Lodge wanted to visit my studio on Stara Street. He came on Saturday. My mother served tea and Napoleon cakes, which she had baked herself. I remember her carefully putting out the dessert on a long table in the kitchen. In return for her hospitality, Lodge brought a box of chocolates, a bottle of French cognac, and a bouquet of compliments about her talented son. Before leaving, he bought a couple of pictures.

That night at 1:00 a.m. I was awakened by the ringing of the telephone.

"How are you, sir?" a faintly squeaky voice inquired.

"Not too bad."

"That's good," the voice squeaked on. "I'm a great admirer of yours, sir."

"That's wonderful, sir," I replied, "but do I have to discover this at one o'clock in the morning?"

"Mr. Kupczynski, we must meet. I would love it if you could meet us at the Ministry of the Interior on Rakowiecka Street."

"I don't have the time. I work very hard to put bread on the table. If you wish to see me, you can come to the Barbakan."

The voice chilled somewhat. "Would you prefer that we send a few of our boys?"

That was enough to alarm me, even though I did not have a guilty conscience. Granted, I'd been trading in foreign currency obtained by selling my paintings, but the authorities had always turned a blind eye to that.

"What time should I be there?" I asked.

"10:00 a.m., and be sure to bring your citizenship card," squeaked the voice in the receiver.

My mother came into the room and said, "What kind of friends are calling you at this hour? Calling like that in the middle of the night! Don't they know that people need to sleep?"

I explained everything to her.

"Be careful, my son," she said. "Those types do not joke around."

29

Troubled by this phone call, I could not fall asleep. I tossed from side to side through the night. Soon after I finally dozed off, the sun woke me up. While I ate breakfast, my mother warned me again to be careful.

"Don't worry, mother," I said. "They won't do anything to me. But if I'm not back in the next few hours, take the case with the money to Auntie Lusia."

Then I left to catch a bus for downtown. After getting off at Nowy Swiat (New World), I walked down Jorozolimska Avenue to get to the tram stop that would take me to Rokowiecka Street. Getting off there I spotted the grey building of the Secret Police immediately. A soldier with a rifle was guarding the gate. He checked my papers and let me pass. As I made my way toward the front doors of the building, I noticed that all the windows were covered with iron bars.

"Papers please," said a vermin-like face from behind a counter. I complied.

"Kupczynski, Zbigniew," the man said without lifting his eyes from a folder full of papers. "First floor. Room number three."

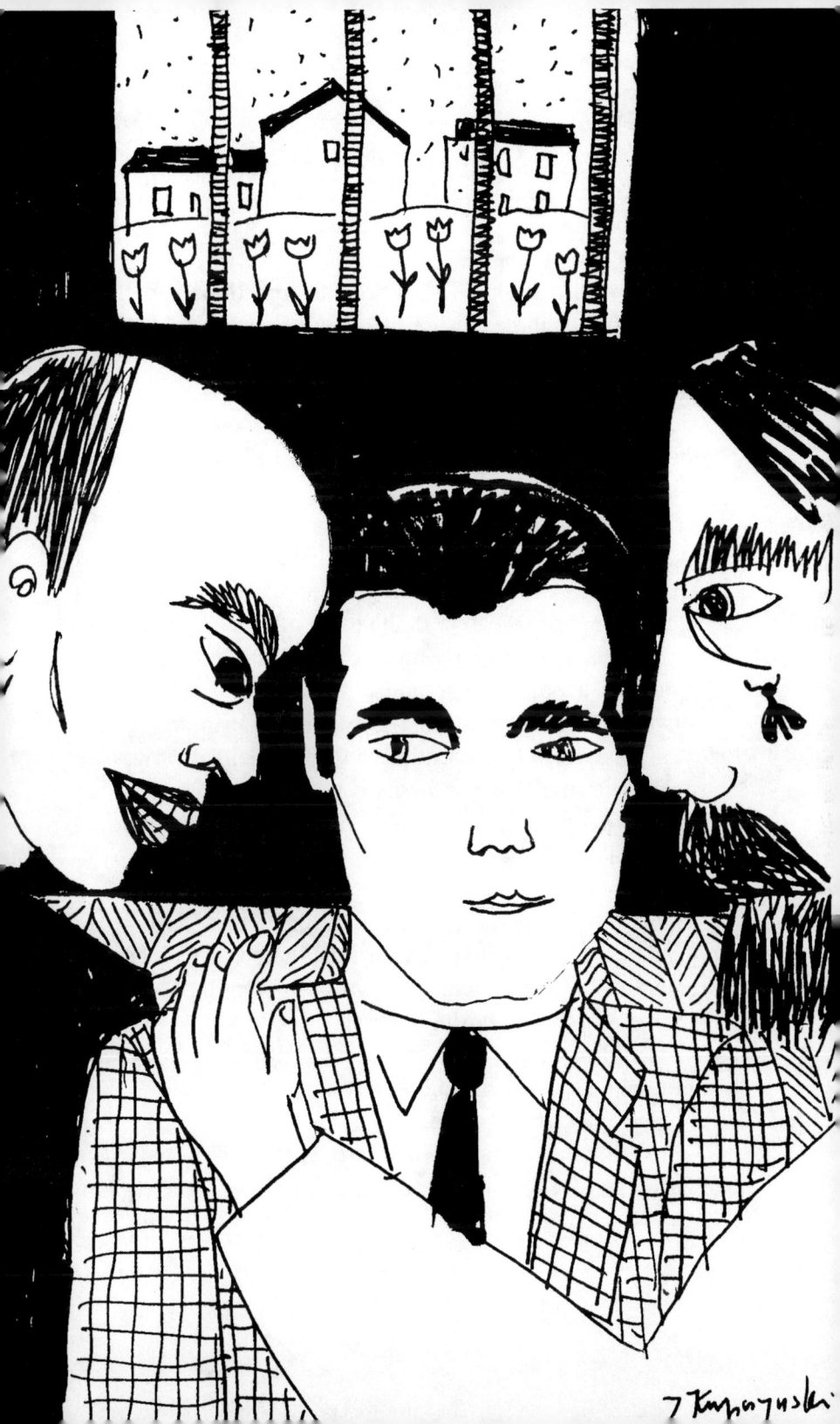

I asked for my identification back.

"We'll be keeping it for the time being," he said, finally looking up, thus revealing a pair of cold eyes and a dark mole on his left cheek.

I ran up a flight of stairs to the first floor and found room number three. Inside were two chairs, a table and a sofa. The windows were barred. I sat on the sofa. After half an hour I started feeling uneasy. I began to pace the room back and forth. At one point I decided I would leave. The doors were locked. I sat in the chair closest to the window. Outside there were chestnut trees and a garbage bin. I picked up a *Trybuna Ludu* (The People's Tribune) from the table. The front page featured an article about the Soviet Army, which was helping our soldiers to put out a fire at a State Farming Collective in the town of Przezdziadka.

Suddenly, two men entered the room, a small blond type with a pointy nose and a seven-foot giant with an apish face. They both wore grey suits that looked clean, even elegant, but I soon detected the smell of unwashed socks. The small man smiled.

"Mr. Kupczynski," he said, "I always knew we would meet one day."

"How was Paris?" asked the giant ape.

"Good," I replied. "Paris is a beautiful city."

"Oh, we're so glad that your time there was well spent," remarked the small man. "We've been wanting to inquire whom you ran into during your stay."

"I did not have the pleasure of chatting with Picasso, but then he's quite difficult to track down."

The ape started laughing.

"Well, you surely met other artists," said the small man, getting up and walking toward me. He showed me a photo from Montmartre. "Who is this man with an umbrella?"

"A Russian Prince, Ivan Ursov. I painted his portrait."

"Not a wise thing to do, Mr. Kupczynski," he said as he glanced knowingly at the ape.

"This man is an American spy. He visited Poland for the Peace Congress. On that occasion his name was Zigfried Shultz."

"He's definitely a playboy," I said, "but a spy?" I shook my head in disagreement, thinking of the time Ursov had taken me to the Bois de Boulogne for a horse race in which four of his stallions were competing.

"And even if he were a spy, what would he want with me? I'm not a general or a minister. I don't know any state secrets."

The interrogation lasted for another half hour, during which time they asked me about every person I had been in contact with in Paris, including Zbyszek Cybulski, Father Gogol and Zdzice Majtczak. To my surprise, they said nothing about the Barbakan. Finally, they let me go. As we parted, the small man offered me some advice.

"You should keep a journal. Then we wouldn't need to bring you in."

"Don't count on me to be your informer," I fired back.

Back on Rakowiecka Street, I walked quickly, wanting to get as far away as possible from the stench of the Secret Police.

30

With the cold of November, everyone deserted the Barbakan, so we stopped exhibiting our work. Having nothing better to do, I began to spend my days in the cafeteria at the headquarters of the Association of Polish Visual Artists. One day Stasio Kiszak sat at my table there and told me about an upcoming painting exhibition that was going to take place alongside a conference on the fine arts.

"Take a look at this," he said, pulling an invitation from his pocket. "They didn't give you one?"

Furious, I ran to the Secretariat. Wilimowska was busy talking with the head of the Adjudication Committee, Professor Wlodyka.

"Why didn't I get an invitation?" I demanded.

Wlodyka passed Wilimowska a knowing glance.

"Isn't your Barbakan show keeping you busy enough? Besides, you're still young. You have plenty of time on your side."

I was dying to punch him out right then and there. Until very recently, he had been churning out Socialist-Realist kitsch. Since the thaw, however, he had suddenly emerged as a great abstractionist and philosopher. I slammed the door and ran outside.

Craving a strong cup of coffee, I dropped into the State Publishing Institute on Foksal Street. The whole literary world gathered there, along with a few visual artists like myself. At the entrance, I was greeted by Jas Himilsbach's crooked smile.

"You still drop in for coffee?" he said. "Why not spot me half a litre of beer instead?"

Looking at Jas's toothless grin, I felt my anger slip away. We walked over to the Mordownia for a beer. A few hours later we left, walking on shakier legs but feeling much better than when we had entered.

Early the next day, I paid a visit to the organizers of the exhibition of the Krzywe Kolo Gallery. These included Bogusz, Kaletan Sosnowski, and Antek Piszczak, the chairman of the Regional Committee for Promotion of Fine Arts who had denounced his own mother in the time of martial law for listening to Radio Free Europe. When I asked them why I had not been selected to exhibit at the gallery, Piszczak laughed at me and said, "you are the director of an open-air circus called the Barbakan!" His jibe gave me an idea: I would stage another open-air show of my own.

One hour before the opening of the Krzywe Kolo exhibition, I placed a dozen or so colourful paintings on the wall of the gallery. Now all I needed was some artificial light, for it was getting dark. Fortunately, I received an unexpected visit from Gienek, a notorious drunk who, by some miracle, had taken an enormous liking to my paintings. When I told him about my predicament, he promptly stole a few floodlights from a nearby construction site and set them up to shine on my work. Andek Drunda did his part by hiring a taxi for three hours and stocking its back

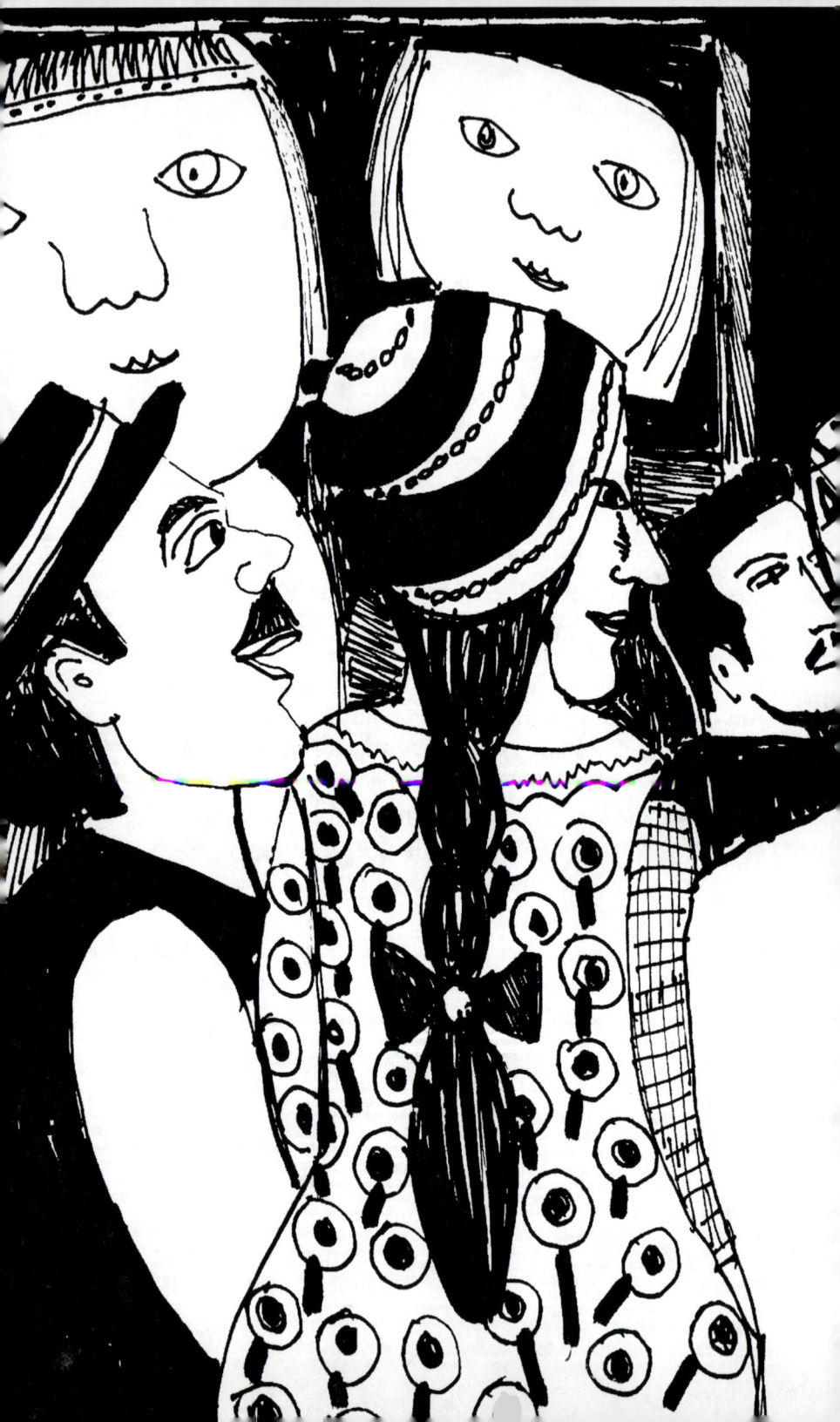

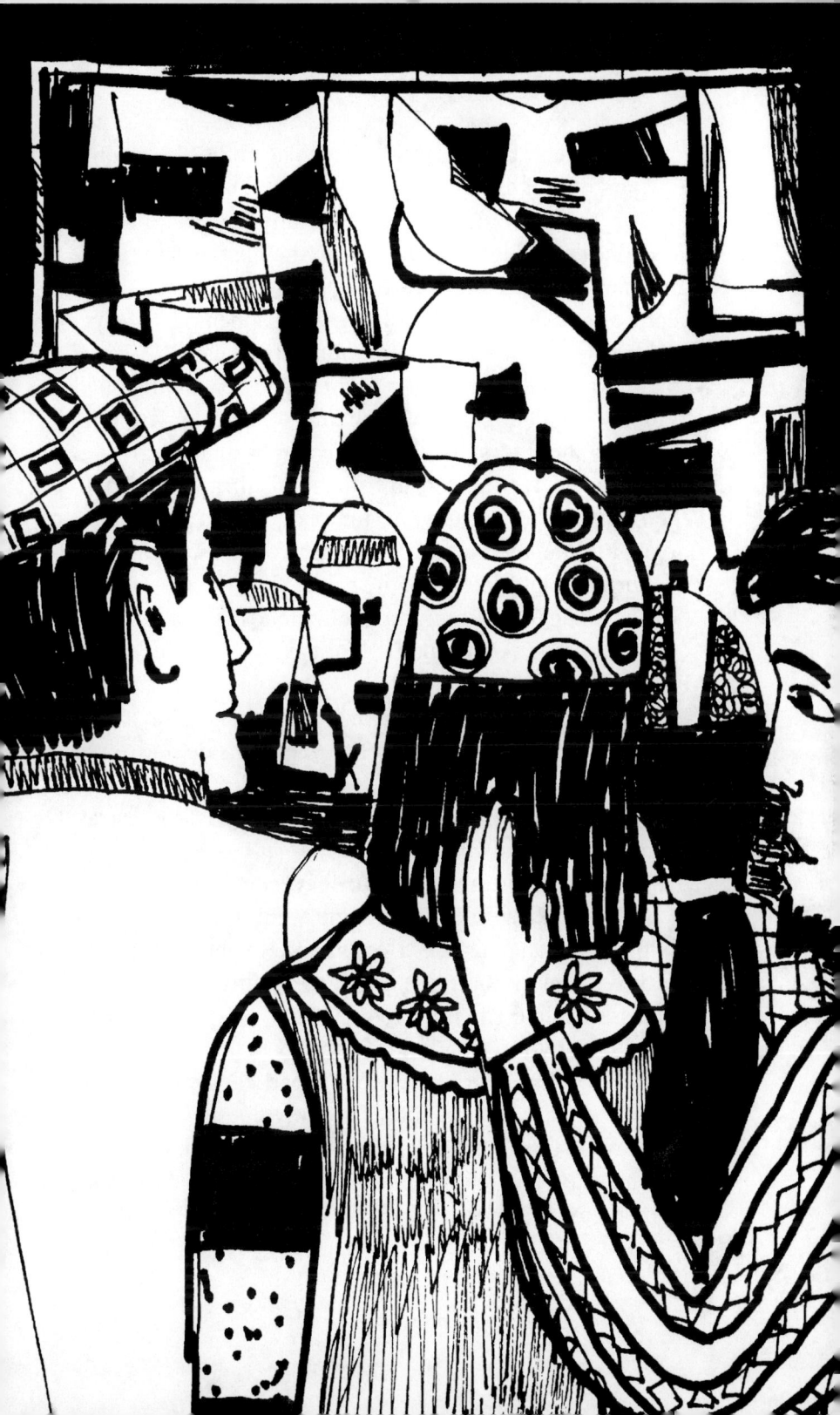

seat with several bottles of Select Vodka, some glasses and a few jars of pickles.

Everything we needed for a good party was now in place. With my paintings glowing in the glare of the floodlights like precious stones, we began to sip the vodka. The street was still dead quiet. Nothing was happening. Silence. Then we heard the hum of an approaching car. When the vehicle arrived, several people got out. Their clothes had obviously been bought abroad and most had cameras slung over their shoulders. Their leader was a man wearing a leather coat. I recognized him to be Chairman Piszczak. When he saw my pictures he jumped. Then a tall, clean-shaven, middle-aged man walked up to a red painting.

"Formidable. I like this," he said.

Others began motioning to their friends.

"Wunderbar Austellung!" squeaked the director of Munich museum.

Soon the party was in full swing. Thoroughly irritated, Piszczak tried his best to herd my guests inside and up to the first floor of the gallery.

"The art upstairs is a hundred times better," Piszczak hissed.

My guests were reluctant to leave my paintings, but they followed Piszczak's urging and went upstairs, leaving me alone. Half an hour later Bogusz and Kajatan Sosnowski stumbled down the staircase drunk as a pair of monkeys.

"It's a terrible shame, Zbyszek, that everything ended so quickly for you," they said with tears in their eyes.

"Not to worry," I told them. "The party has just begun."

I was right. A few minutes later, my guests were back. Gienio was soon busy pouring glasses of vodka while I distributed the pickles. Later that evening a tall American sat down beside me on a bench.

"My name is Bernard Davis," he said. "I'm the president of the Museum of Modern Art in Miami. I'll buy the whole lot."

Bogusz almost had a stroke. Kajatan was too drunk to react. The curator of the Krzywe Kolo show, who was standing close by when the offer was made, ran away. The following day Bernard Davis turned up at my house. After examining my pictures closely, he chose twenty of the best, including the ones I had shown the night before. He paid me two thousand dollars in hundred dollar bills. Then we shared a bottle of plum wine and shook hands like good friends.

"What are you planning to do with all this money?" My mother's voice had a note of jealousy.

"I'll stash it in my bag and let it sit there. For now we've got enough to get by on. Maybe I'll go skiing in Zakopane."

The winter, it turned out, was long and cold. Instead of going to the mountains, as I had hoped, I bought oil paints and started a series of Malgosia's portraits using primarily black and white. The winter, with its thick white flakes falling endlessly from the sky, had made me melancholy.

To cheer myself up, I bought a boxer pup that I named Antek. Within two months he was too rambunctious and strong for my mother to walk.

You should buy a warm coat for Malgosia. It will be winter soon; she'll catch a cold in that little windbreaker from Paris."

"All right, mother," I answered.

My divorce from Renata had been final for some time. We had never been able to resolve our difficulties, which were always made worse by the constant interference of my mother-in-law.

31

Then I met Ewa, a beautiful girl with black hair and large blue eyes. She liked my work, Malgosia and Atek. Looking at her, I felt that she was a woman who would accompany me in good times and bad until the end of my life.

From the time we met, Ewa and I went everywhere together, two inseparable lovebirds. Having travelled to Zakopane (Poland's most famous ski resort) and Masury (Poland's lake district), we got married in Zaduszki on All Hallows Eve. Ours was a small civil ceremony attended by only our parents and two neighbours, Delinkajtys and Miss Basia. I must confess that I forgot to buy the wedding bands, an omission for which it would take my wife several years to forgive.

Ewa soon had our first child. The two of them would often come to visit me at the Barbakan, which was once again up and running. On one occasion Tadeusz Rolke, a photojournalist from Stolica, took a picture of the three of us there: a young family against a background of ancient stone walls and modern art.

Some months later, Bernard Davis turned up in Warsaw once again, bringing with him a catalogue from my show in the Miami Museum of Modern Art, which had received some good reviews. He had sold a few of my paintings and was interested in buying some more. This time he paid four thousand for only fifteen works, three of which were fairly large.

Once again my success led to an interrogation on Rakowiecka Street. As before, I was obliged to surrender my papers at the counter. This time, however, I was taken to a different room. The lights there were apparently not working so I sat there in the pitch black with the doors locked, for three long hours, impatiently waiting for the small blond man and the giant ape to appear. Finally I heard footsteps in the hall. A key rattled in the lock and the small man entered, followed by the ape. To my surprise, the lights came on, blinding me for a while.

"Zbyszek, it's nice to see you," said the small man. "I've been reading about your successes in *The New York Times*. Congratulations."

He held out his skinny hand. I could see that he had put on some weight. And he must have put on some new socks, since I could not smell his feet. He asked if I wanted coffee. When I shook my head to decline, he told me I could go home.

"We had intended to ask you about a few things, but in the meantime we found them out through other means."

I sighed in relief and returned to the Barbakan where Smola confided that he too had been summoned to Rakowiecka. The authorities, he said, wanted to know if I was selling a lot to foreigners.

"And what did you tell them?" I asked.

"That you weren't," he replied with a note of irony in his voice—his way of acknowledging that my works were selling well indeed.

32

The year that followed my second visit to Rakowiecka Street was filled with the joys and frustrations of family life. Beata, with her lovely round face and blue eyes, started walking, filling her parents with pleasure and pride. My mother, however, regarded the child with displeasure. She was upset that I had remarried and then had a second child with Ewa. She began sticking her nose into our business. Constant arguments erupted at home. My mother favoured Malgosia at every turn. She slipped her treats, bought her imported dresses, and pampered her. As a result, Malgosia began neglecting her schoolwork and irritated her teachers by, among other things, showing up to class with polished fingernails. Ewa tried everything to win Malgosia's affection, but her attempts were in vain; my mother always succeeded in turning my daughter against her.

At the Barbakan, things continued to go well. One day, about a year after my second visit to Rakowiecka Street, a Dane by the name of Werner Kargard came to announce that he wanted to hold an exhibition of my work in Copenhagen. He bought a few dozen pictures and said he would need more.

"I must have at least thirty pictures," he told me. "It would be best if you came to paint the remainder at my house in Denmark. I'll supply the paints, brushes, canvases, and my wife—an excellent cook—will produce the meals. Since you paint quickly, in two months you'll have the paintings we need for our exhibition. Then we'll rent a gallery, organize an opening, and split the profits fifty-fifty. What do you say?"

This kind of proposition was not to be taken for granted, especially since the supply of money I stored in the suitcase under my bed was rapidly shrinking. My financial situation had become so precarious, in fact, that I had even been toying with the idea of applying to the Ministry of Culture for a grant. Werner had turned up at the perfect moment.

"You've got a deal," I said. "When do I leave?"

Using the money that Werner had left for the purpose, I purchased my ticket for the flight and applied for a passport. Parting from Ewa and my daughters was difficult. They accompanied me to the airport, where I hugged and kissed them goodbye. Moved to tears and wanting to hide my sorrow, I ran to the departures ramp.

Moments later I was buckled securely in my seat, looking out of the window at the massive wing that flexed up and down as we rumbled down the runway. When we rose above the clouds and reached our desired elevation, I unbuckled my seat belt and gazed at the scene below. Everything was drowning in milky white haze.

At the airport in Copenhagen I was greeted by rain. Werner, wearing a grey trench coat with an upturned collar, was waiting to greet me.

"Welcome to Denmark," he said with a smile.

The drive to Werner's home took no time at all. When

we reached the highway, he pushed the pedal quickly to the floor and held it there until the speedometer hit 140 kilometres per hour. As the countryside whizzed by, my host hummed an aria from "Rigoletto."

His home, located on the outskirts of Copenhagen, was beautiful. I especially enjoyed its sunny terrace and large garden, where his three blond, blue-eyed children liked to play. Niklas, the youngest son, showed a considerable interest in colour. From the very first day of my stay, he watched attentively from the back of his wooden horse as I spread the paints on my canvas. I reciprocated by painting a good likeness of him that greatly pleased his mother.

When I tried to paint little Nicolette, the daughter, I was less successful. Her very regular features gave me a lot of trouble. In the end, I painted over her image in frustration and turned the canvas into a grey abstraction. Werner was pleased to let me go my way, and I used my freedom to paint simple but strange figures, part children, part monsters, that were somewhat reminiscent of primitive paintings. For paint I used mostly shades of grey that shone with a silver or pearly finish. The paintings thus produced evoked the sentiments of a man lost in a fog seeing people with three or four eyes but without lips.

My show, which took place inside a small but very elegant gallery in downtown Copenhagen, attracted a lot of attention. Twenty paintings were sold in the course of the first week. Rolf Knulson, a local critic, wrote a fairly comprehensive article about a painter from beyond the Iron Curtain, who was hiding from the Communists in a mist of Freudian dreams. "Very strange painting," he wrote, "a mixture of melancholy and dark humour. Work that one cannot forget."

I met Knulson one evening for dinner in a local restaurant. He ate his fish greedily, as if he had not seen food for three days. In between bites he found time to tell me that success turned a man into an animal while suffering made him an artist.

"Your strength," he said, looking intensely at me through his horn-rimmed glasses, "depends on the survivor's instinct that you've developed in response to Communism."

Looking at his beady eyes, I had the urge to burst out laughing. Western criticism of art was rife with this nonsense, which is an integral part of the reigning cult of suffering. If Abakanowicz had not churned out work on Auschwitz, she would have had a much harder time achieving fame. The same goes for Gorecki and his music. The darker the vision, the more people are inclined to believe that the work produced is genuine art.

I drove home to Warsaw in my new Volvo with enough money in my pocket to support my family for two years. I felt a sense of pride as my first trip to a Scandinavian country was a big success. My car passed many cars, relentlessly devouring the highway as I drove with the excessive speed of an overconfident, novice driver. Thankfully luck did not abandon me and I managed to arrive in Warsaw intact.

I drove through Noway Swiat, Krakowskie Przedmiescie and I stopped at Starowka and parked my car at the Barbakan.

Naliwajko was the first to greet me. "The King is back."

"Right," I said as I watched him jealously eye my new Volvo.

"Next year I'll pop over to Sweden and pick one up for myself," he said sardonically.

I exhibited my art at the Barbakan for the next couple of years and continued to be a successful artist. I had the basic luxuries that were hard to come by in a communist country for the average working person; western designer clothing, a decent amount of money and a nice studio in the heart of town. This created a certain degree of jealousy in my rivals. I did not allow myself to be distracted by envious whisperings behind my back and was commissioned to paint two elaborate murals. The first was in Oswiecim in a new cultural centre and the second was a two-hundred-square-metre ceiling mural in another cultural centre in Radomsko.

Christmas was very festive and lavish that year for my family and me. As I watched the snowflakes gently fall from the sky I said to Ewa, "Let's go skiing to Zakopane." And so we did.

In the spring of the following year I landed another exhibition in Stockholm. This time my wife accompanied me. The show was another success: I sold about ten pieces and my art attracted a large, eclectic crowd. One memorable fellow wore a Prussian, pointed, metal helmet and a huge, colorful parrot on his shoulder which had no problem defecating on the hors d'oeuvre table. I remember someone telling me once that bird shit is good luck, so I smiled to myself and didn't let the unappetizing sight of it ruin my evening.

Bernard Davis was not quite finished with me yet. I received word that he had put one of my paintings in the Philadelphia Museum of Modern Art, home of works by Picasso, Klee, Matisse and other very prominent artists. Once again, timing proved to be crucial in my life. I believe that the prominence of this exhibition influenced the Polish government to allow my youngest daughter to join my wife and me in Sweden. Malgosia elected not to join us, but eventually moved to Germany, where she lives today.

Soon after, at the Stockholm airport, we watched our five-year-old daughter walk off the plane wearing a sign on her chest 'Beata Kupczynski.' Tired from the long trip, she slept in my arms on the way to our car.

One year later, in 1970, we immigrated to Canada and so began a new chapter in our lives.

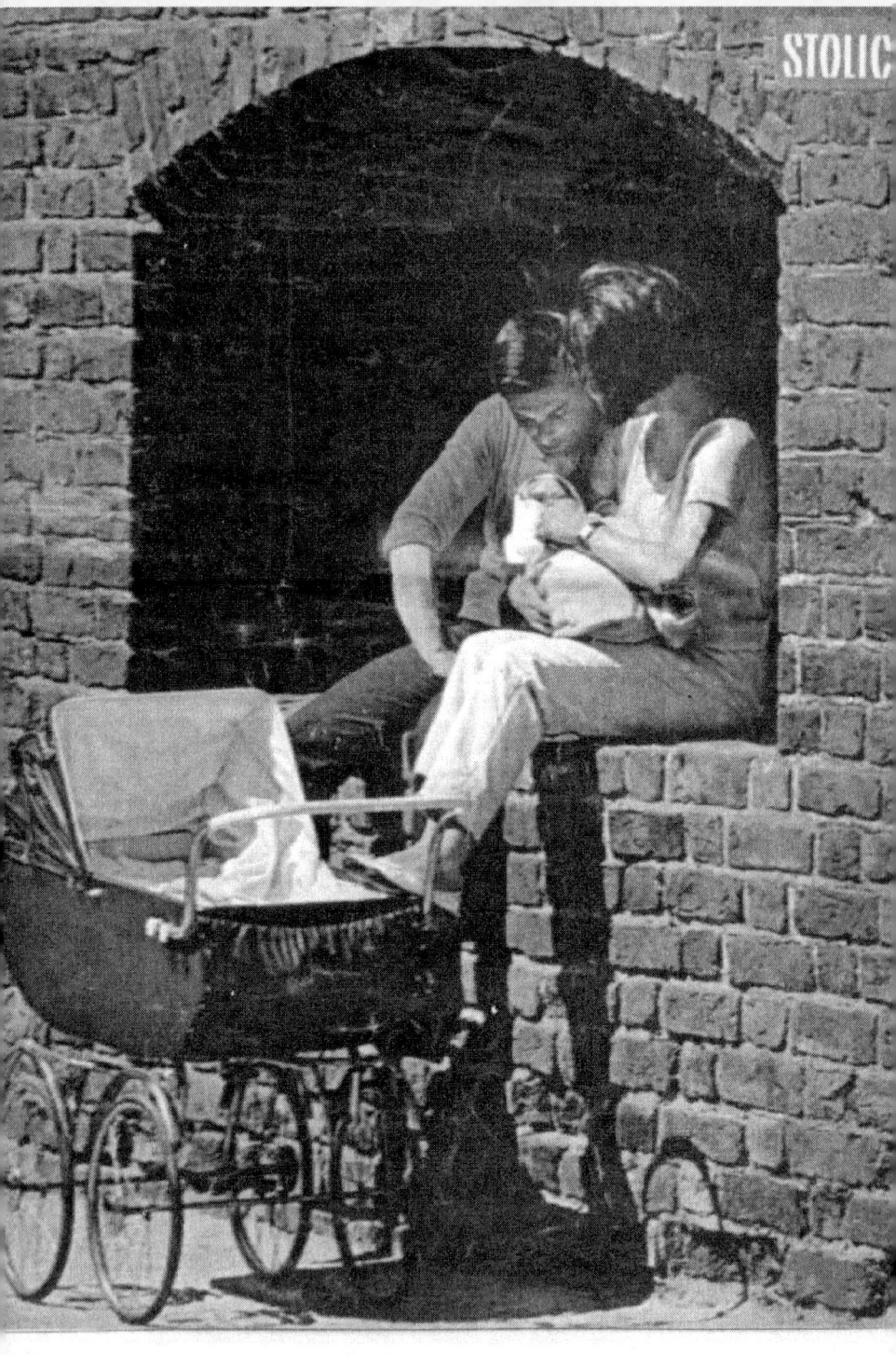

The Kupczynski family at the Barbakan

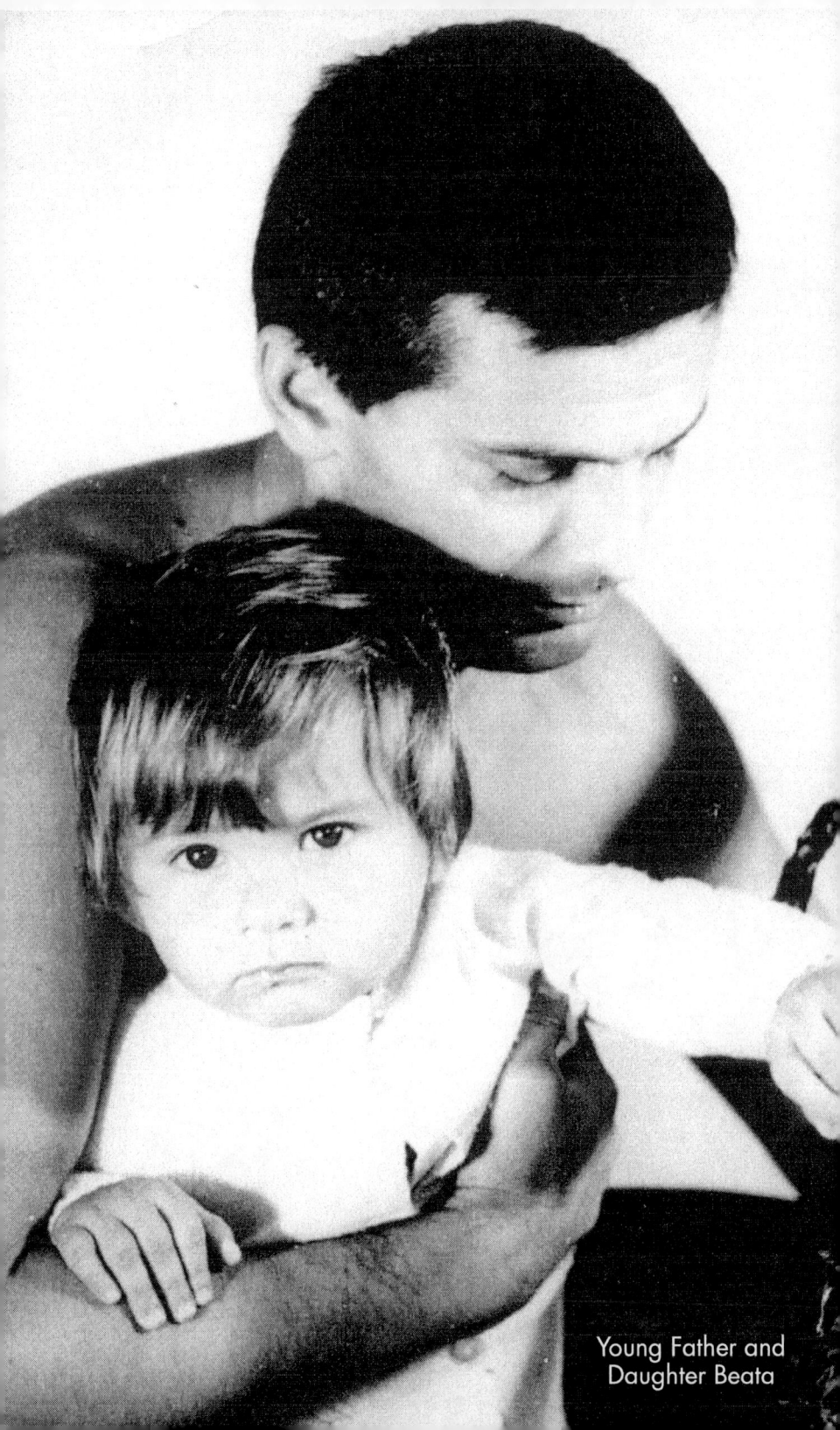

Young Father and Daughter Beata

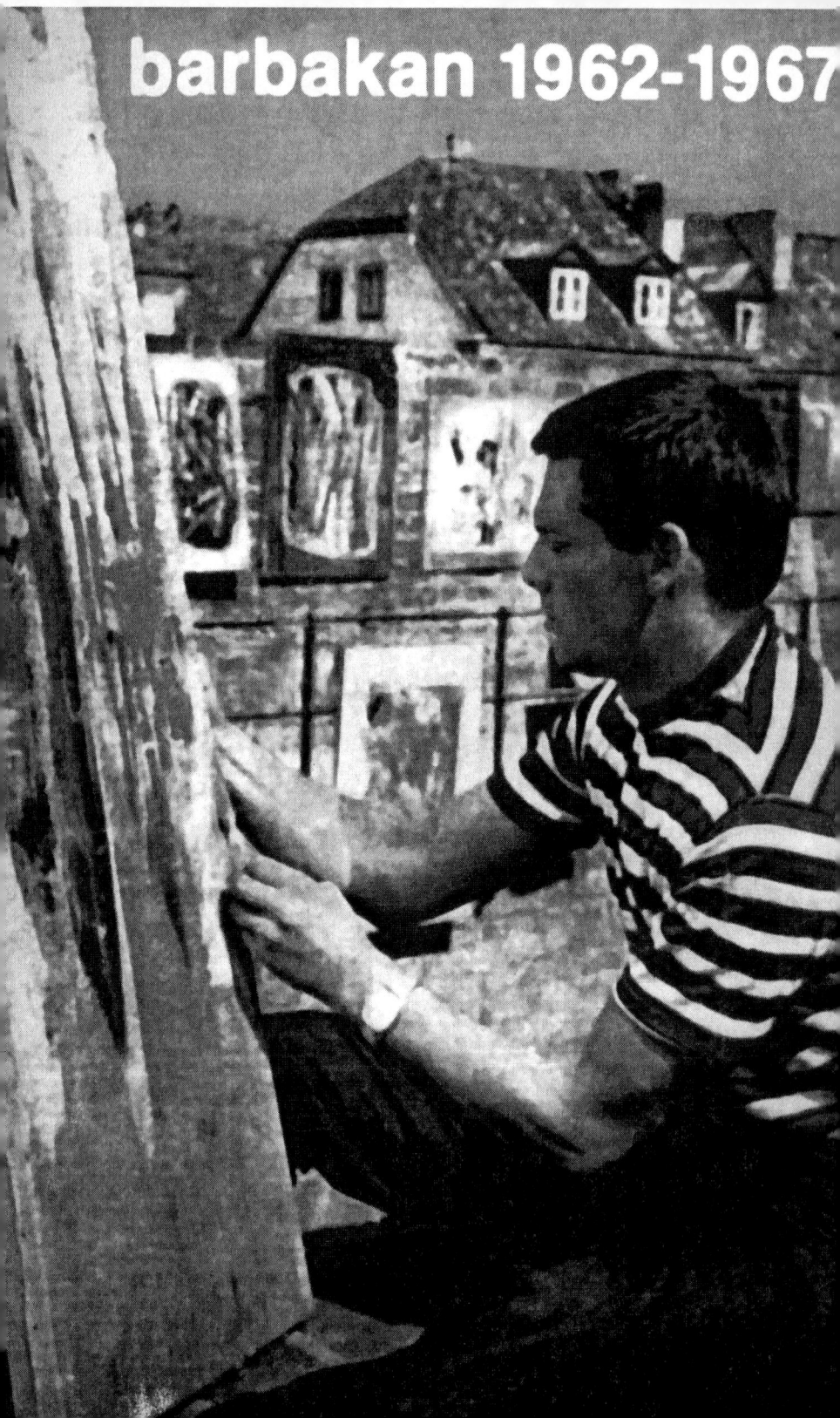

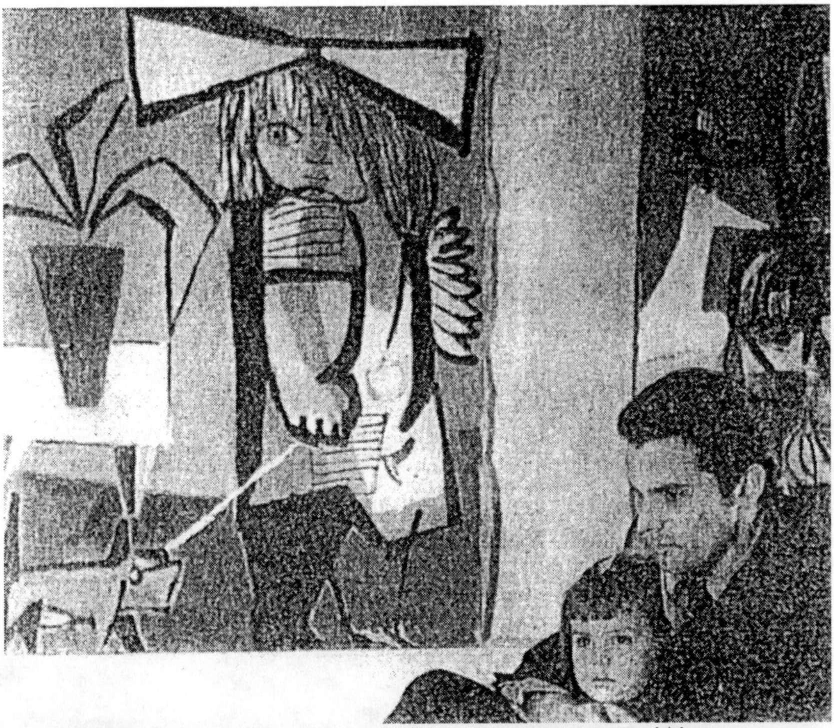

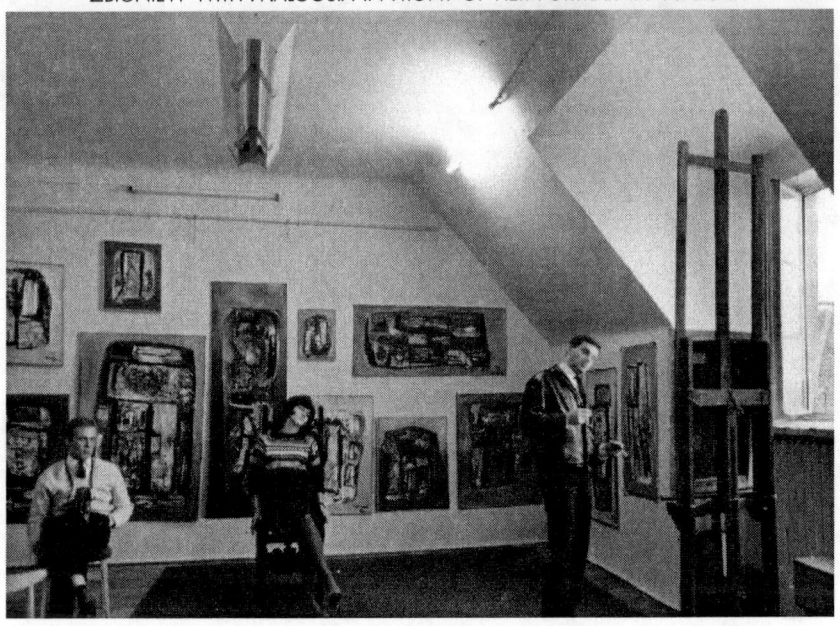

ZBIGNIEW WITH MALGOSIA IN FRONT OF HER PORTRAIT IN WARSAW

KUPCZYNSKI'S STUDIO IN WARSAW

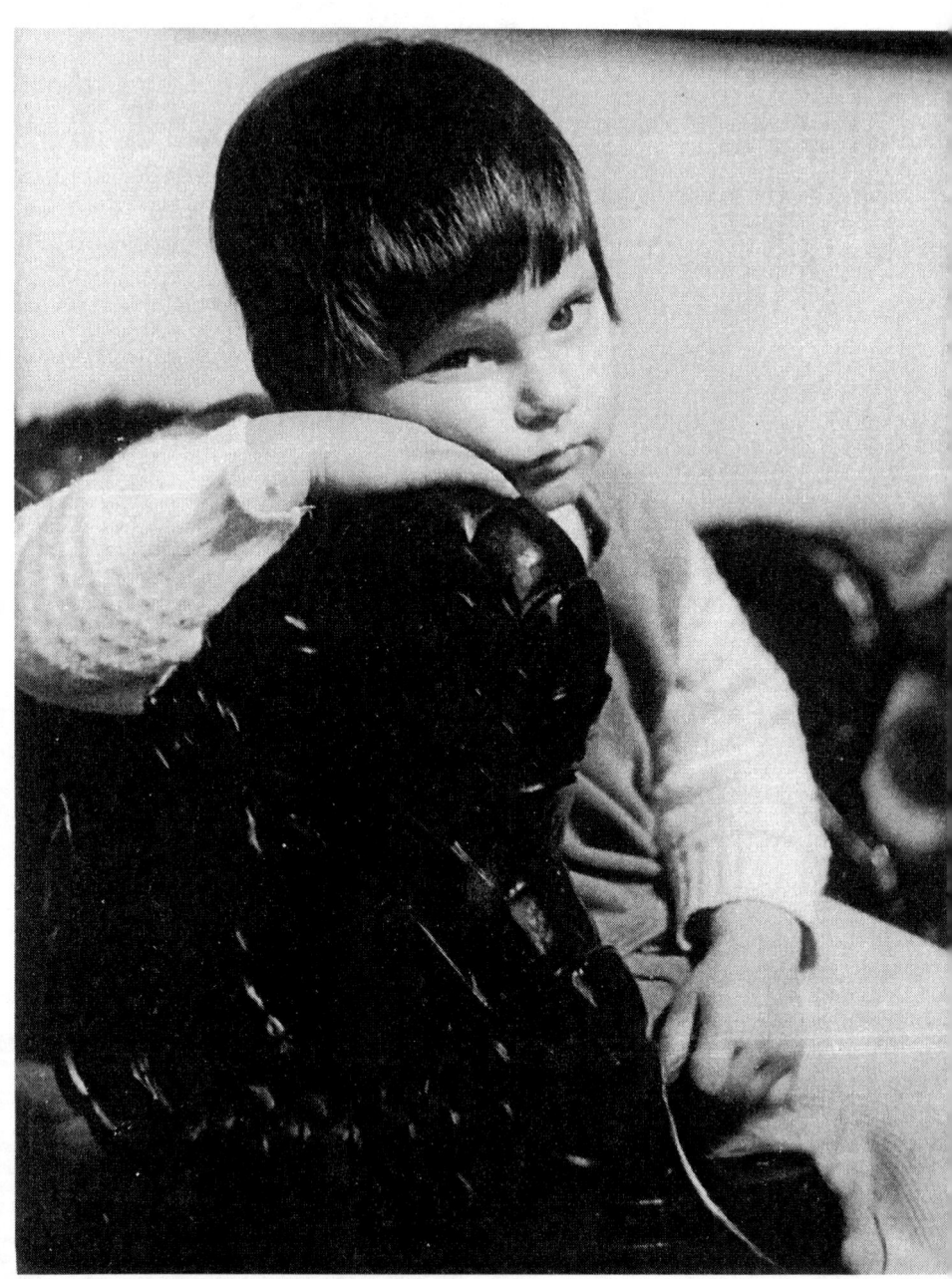

Beata

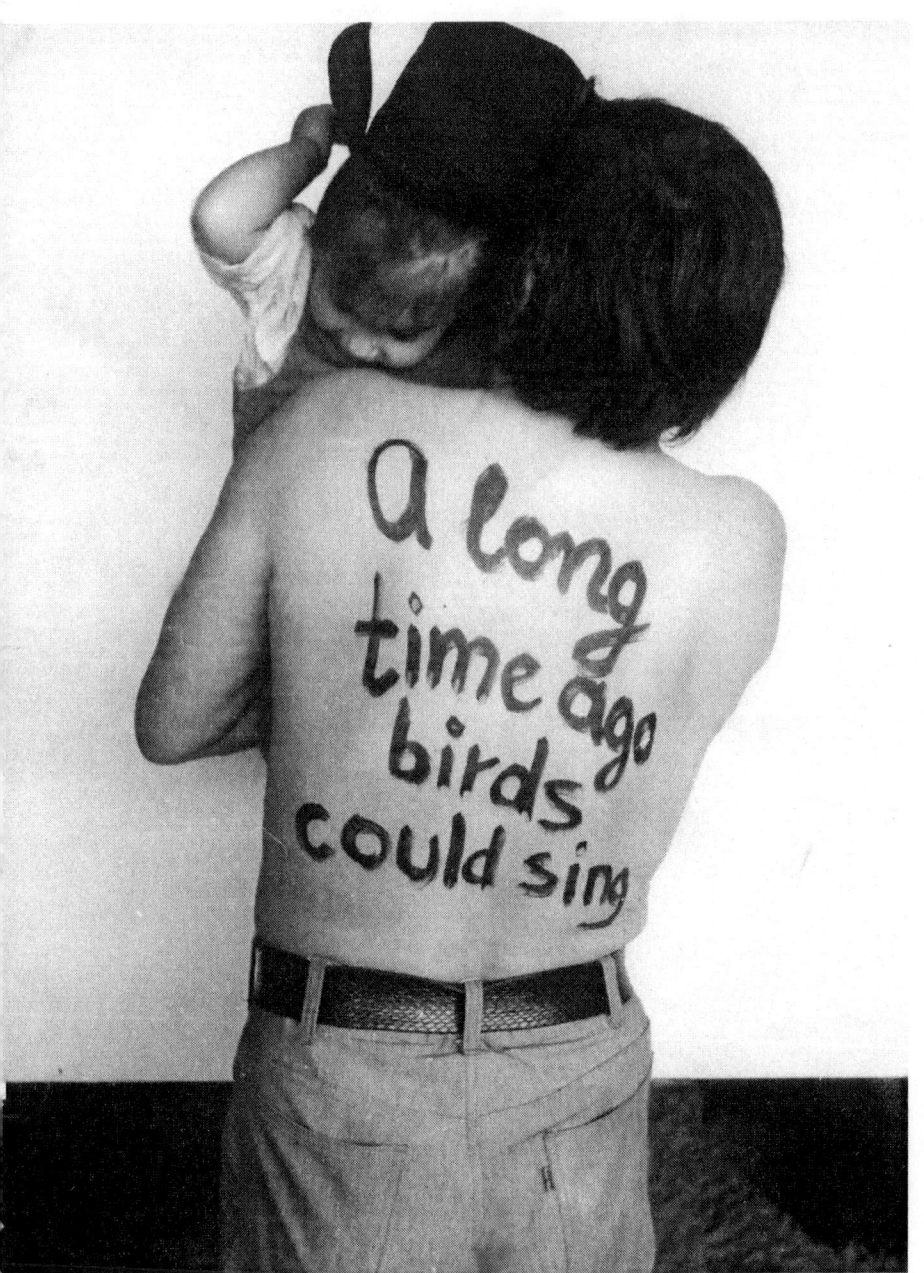

BODY ART

ARTSPEAK

NEW YORK, N.Y.   A TWICE-A-MONTH GALLERY REVEIW   Vol. VI, No. 5, November 1, 198

NOVEMBER GALLERY GUIDELIST

On Capotondi, Greenstein, Havlicek-Tortora, Hutson, Kupczysnki, Raphael. Sculpture, Photography.

The faces of Zbigniew Kupszynsl

Joseph Merkel

The paintings of the Polish Canadian Zbigniew Kupczynski are illuminations. Illuminations to him in his visions, illuminations to the viewer because they describe a world of his experience, a world which combines the folk ways of his native King lost, Poland and those of the Northwest Indians of his home area, Vancouver, with his new life. One sees all this in his solo exhibit of large oil pastels and large paintings at the Carimar Galleries, 20 East 76 Street, November 1 to 12, the debut in New York of this internationally known painter

These works can be described as Folk Art. The style is that of the more simplified Folk Art, all the faces being fully frontal and all the persons, objects and scenes being conventionalised in treatment. African sculpture also has contributed to Kupczynski's manner, especially to the broad nose and the divisions of planes in the face, which make some faces resemble those of Rouault.

The art of borrowing

The Pop artists were the first to demonstrate, in the 60's, how art could borrow from other disciplines, when it took work whole from commercial art, for example, Jasper Johns' beer cans or Campbell soup ever since, there has been a lot of "cross breeding" in the arts, mostly beneficial. This has allowed many artists as inclined to discover that Folk Art is an excellent source of inspiration. Artists of Central Europe have exploited this area a great deal (witness the Hungarian artists in a review of this current issue), especially after the fine example of Marc Chagall.

Another Folk artist of Polish origin with a powerful voice, Kupczynski, can employ this approach to make his personal statement. He takes the same subject matter and the same means but gives each his personal emphasis, thus arriving at a radically different art from Chagall. One ... note each different el... Art as we ...

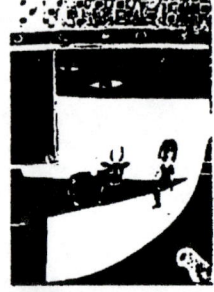

Zbigniew Kupczynski, "The King and I," (detail), Carimar Galleries

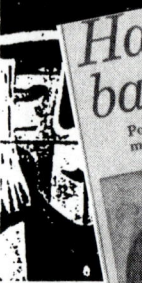

Zbigniew Kupczynski, (detail), Carimar Gallerie

motifs, internationally recognized, fantasy, content, style. A quick summary of how he does this will be followed by a more detailed look at color and fantasy alone:

The paintings and oil pastels

Kupczynski handles color in broad areas with the boldest of contrasts in his large paintings, while in the oil pastels there is more subtlety in rich color and more contrast of broad and patterned areas. Special motifs consist of the facial ones of eyes, noses, lips in every work and of decorative patterns, often geometric, such as the blanket on the red cow's back or "Re Cow at Night," and of flowers, still in the clothing, in the background, all over the blue eyes in the oil paste with the clarinet player. Almost no work lacks a musical instrument or an animal. Except in the clarinet player pastel, where a m... chugging acro...

use of specifically in th... or decoration of the pa... subject itself is usually... inside the house with a... or outdoors with an ani... point of the subject is th... is disproportionately larg... very striking, with its lo... nose, its piercing eyes an... conventionalized lips in ev... colors of the fac...

kredki do reki, gdy w dziewiątym zachodniej na b... dnie się ropnaflu. 17 września 1939 roku arkadia w ciągu paru parafia. Żydów. Najmłej skończyły sobie do komór gazowych.

Rodzinne wiejskiego nauczyciela trafiło się także do Gubernialnego Ge-bernatorstwa - unikali wywiózki na Syberii lub do Kazachstanu. Po wojnie trafili na ziemie odzyskane. Zbigniew rozpoczął studia malarskie we Wrocławiu. Chciał na płótnie ocalić spaloną arkadie. W szkole dowiedział się, że niepobudowane ideały jego marzeń doskonałą kapitalistycznej zamiłuje Szarkadia, to tylko złudzenie, że socjalistycznemu artyście przy... stej malować nie dwuletowe oczer... ty i chasydzkie budnice, lecz trakto-rzystki, dźwigi i przywyskłe na trawi-nach. Dopiero jeden przyszkolę na sia-binizmem. Młodemu artyście wydawa-ło się o zaapentitem praesiziogna-tych profesorów, wie ucieki do sto-lecy. Niestety, nawt tak, Niedobrze i niebezpiecznie było w 1951 roku... irac marzenia do rzeczywistości. "Aby nie malować tych głupot, robiłem to, co mi było wtedy naj-bliższe: zająłem się córką naj-mowieszą kuzią zainteresowała mnie do malowania dzieciątych portre-tów. Moje prace nie mosły się jed-nak w reakach socrealizm. Dopie-ro po zdjęciu ze władzy ogólnopolskiej portrety Małgosi zostały zauważone przez krytykę. Wowczas mistrzo-

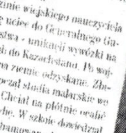

skandynawskiej telewizji nakręciła o mnie doku-dem samochodem Volvo. Te kontakty spowodowa-

---

ALLGEMEINES LEXIKO
DER BILDENDEN KÜNS
DES XX. JAHRHUNDERTS

UNTER MITWIRKUNG VON FACHG... DES IN- UND AUSLAND... BEARBEITET, REDIGIERT UND H... VON
HANS VOLL...

Der berühmte Geiger
Yehudi Menuhin besitzt einen „Kupczynski"

Han skildrer barnesindet

Polsk kunstners udstilling i Horsens imødeses med forventning

Malarz arkadii

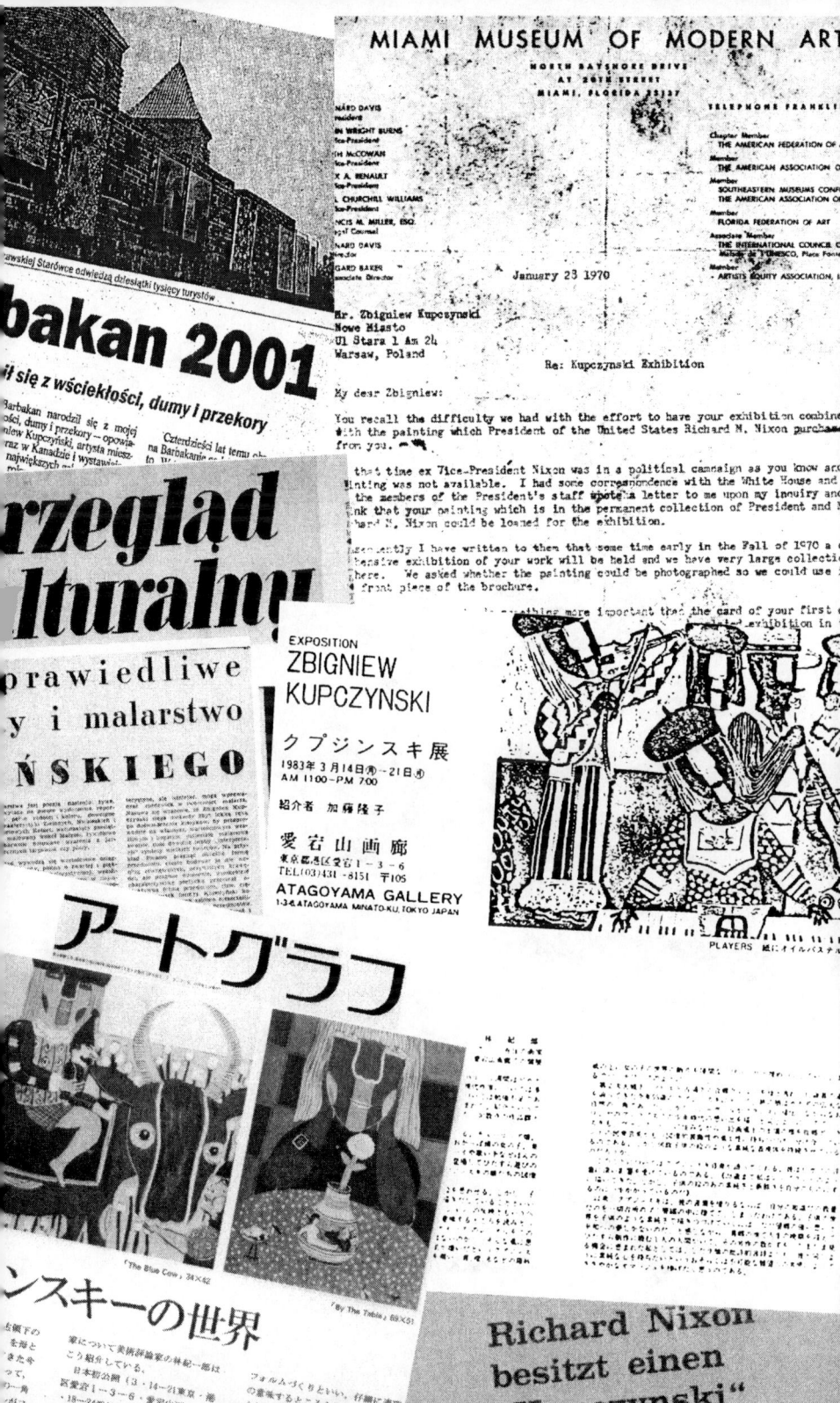

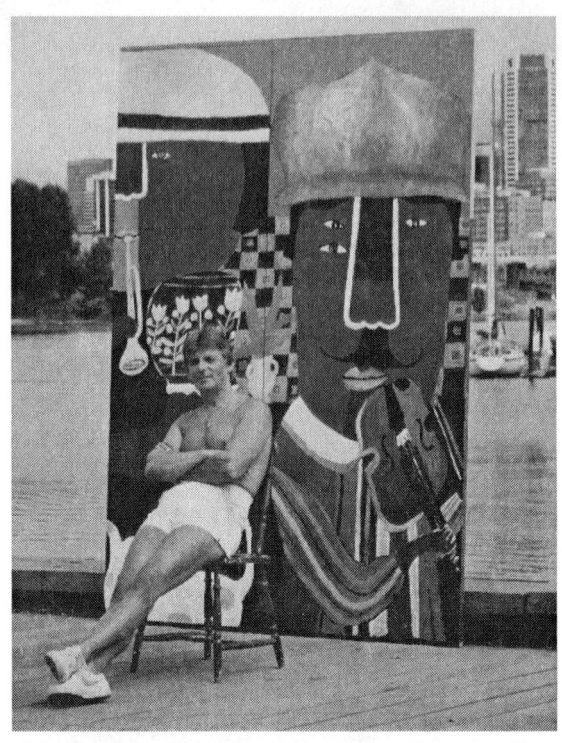

THE ARTIST'S HARD LIFE AT FALSE CREEK

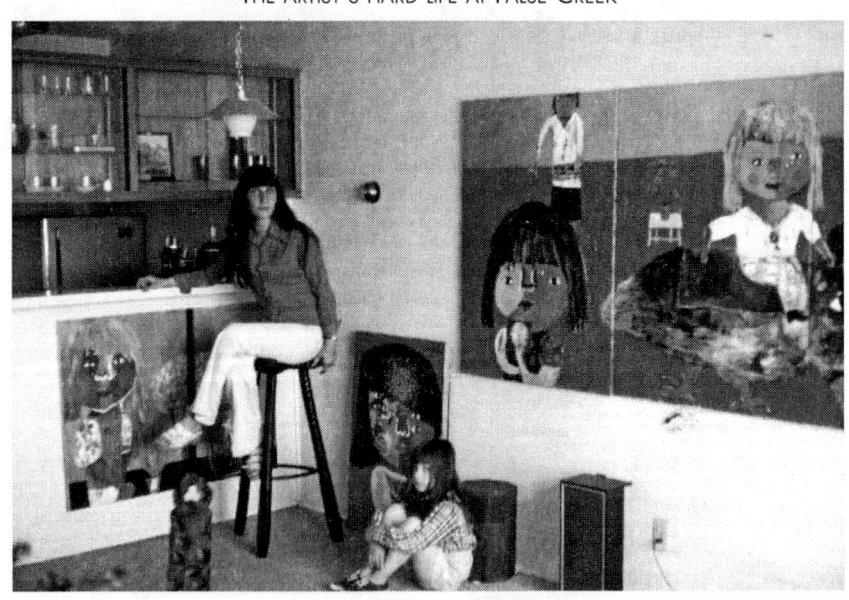

THE FAMILY'S FIRST MONTH IN VANCOUVER

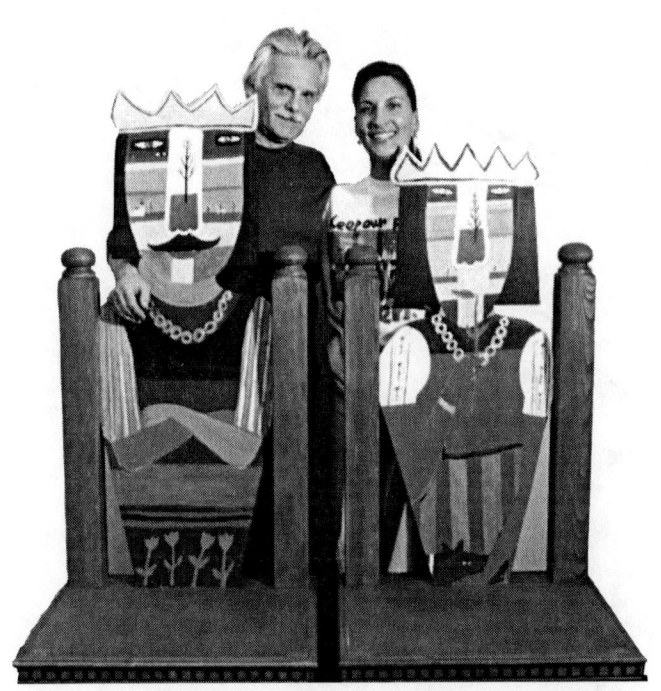

Zbigniew and Eva with chairs

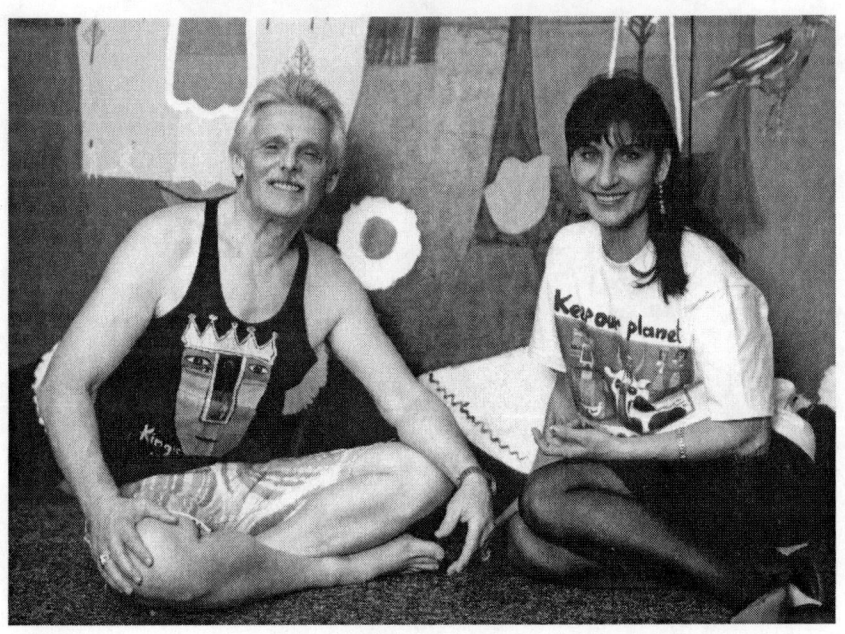

Wearable Art

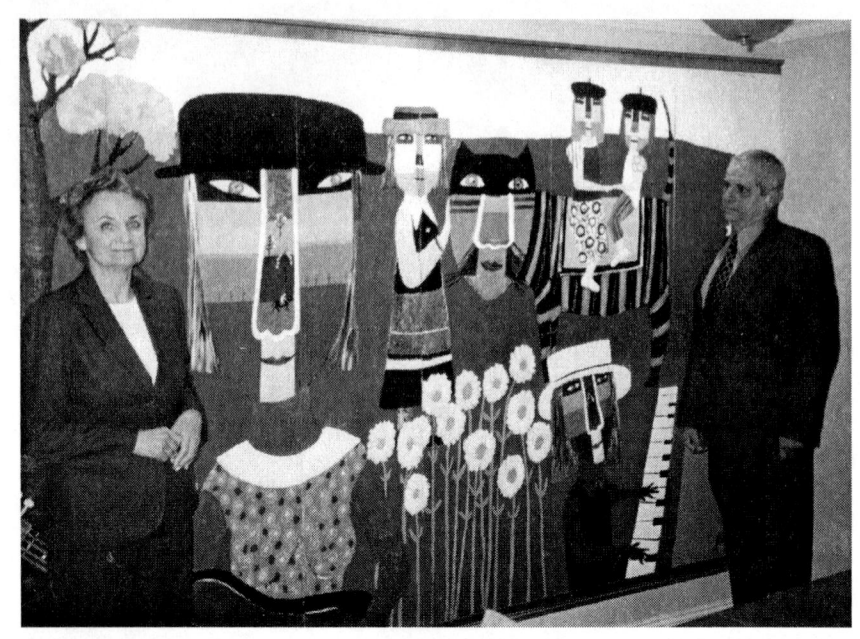

ART PATRONS

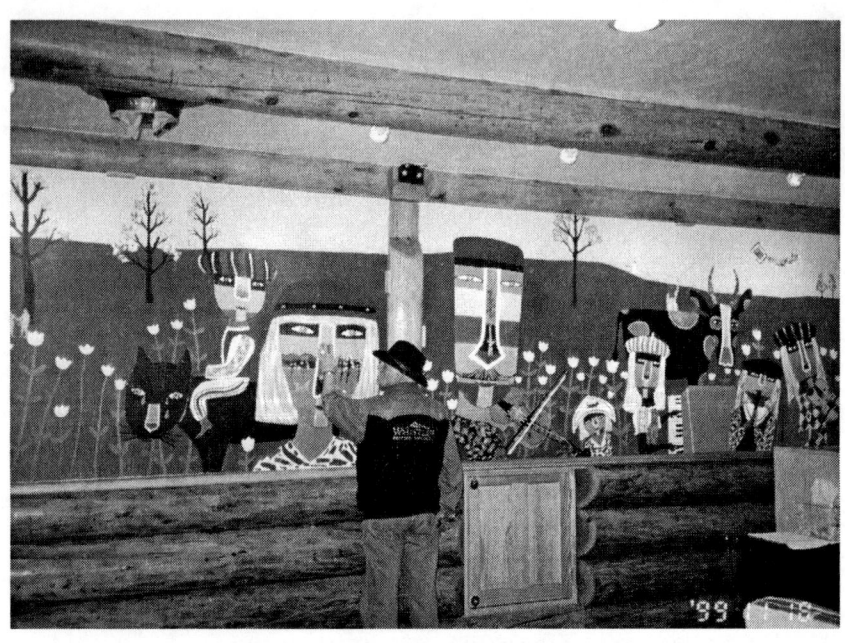

MURAL AT PEMBERTON (NEAR WHISTLER, BC)

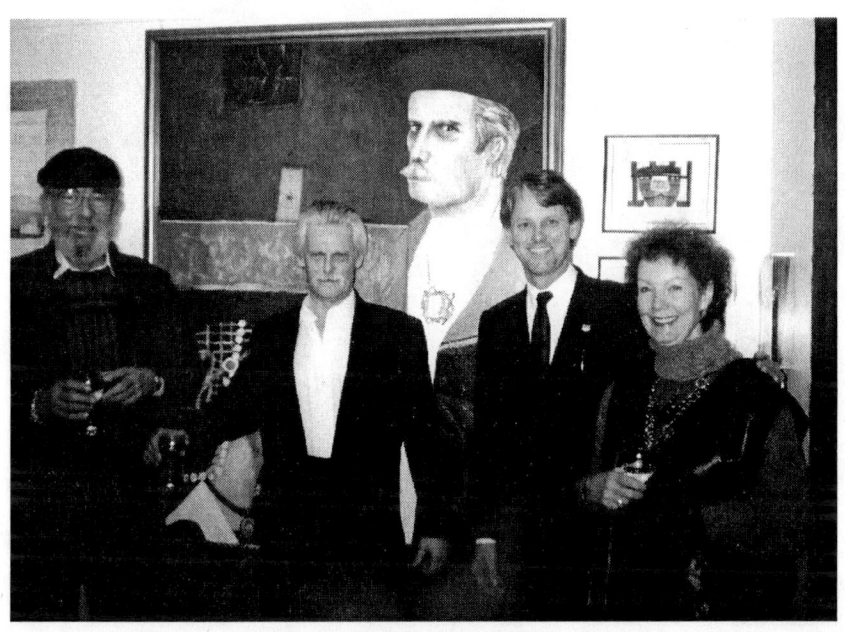

STUDIO VISITORS

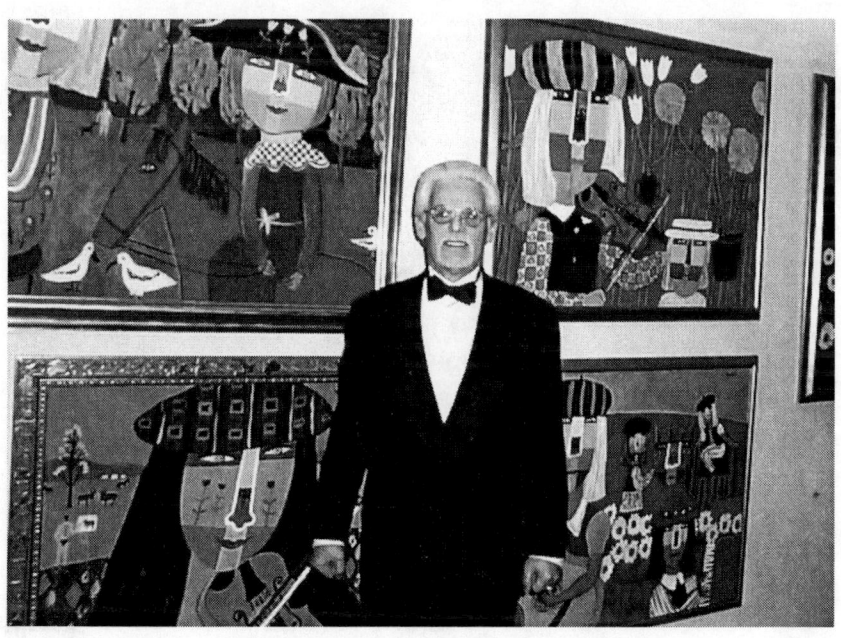

KUPCZYNSKI IN FRONT OF HIS ART WORK

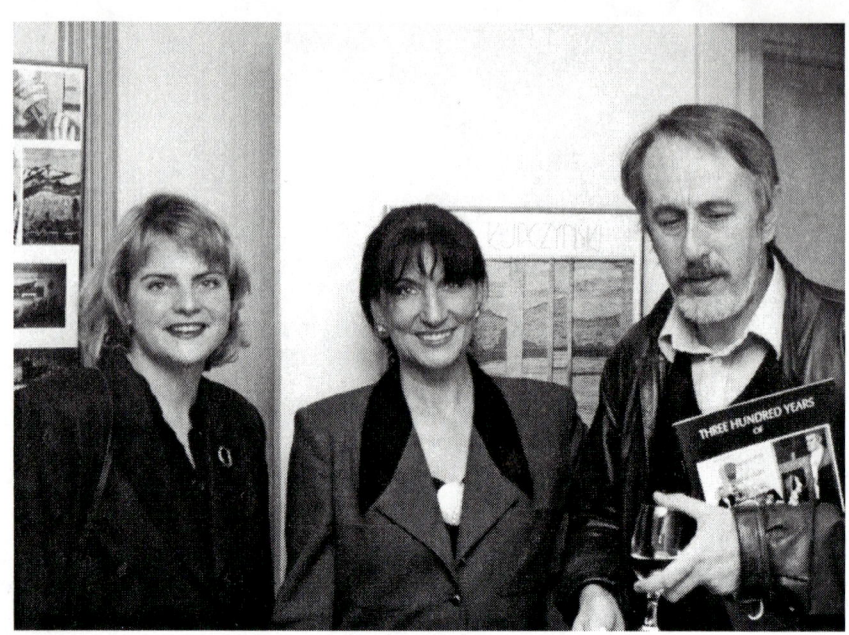

EVA WITH FRIENDS

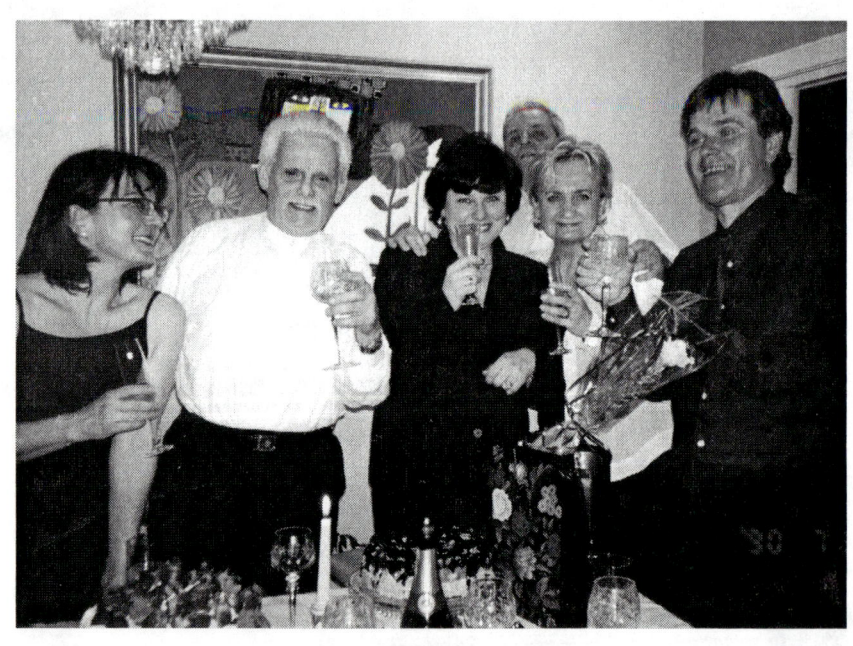

GATHERING AT GALLERY

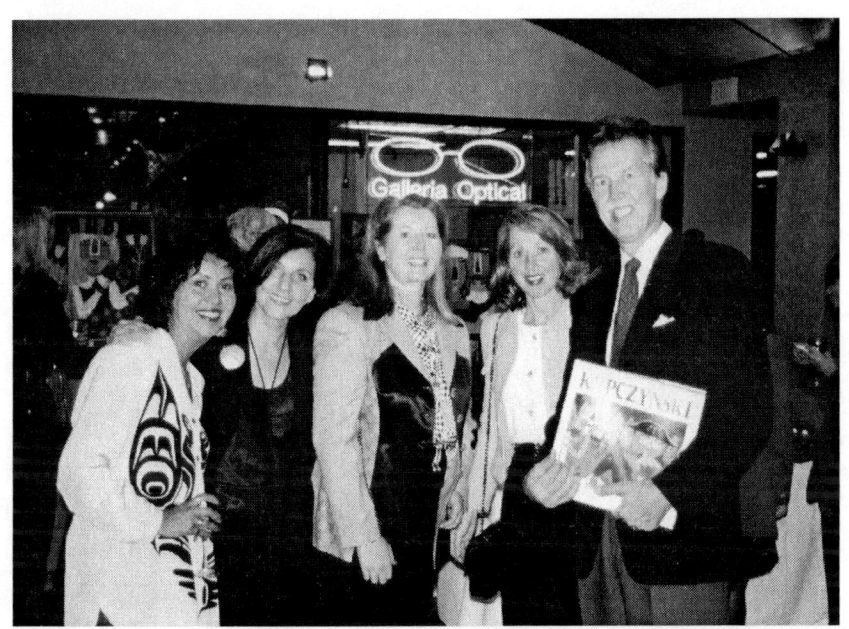

Opening

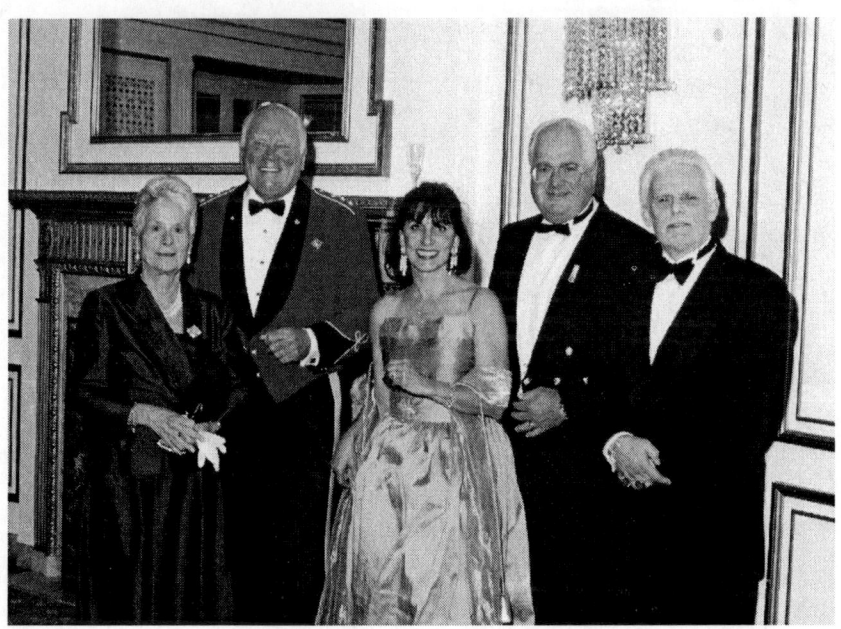

The Kupczynskis with guests

Gallery

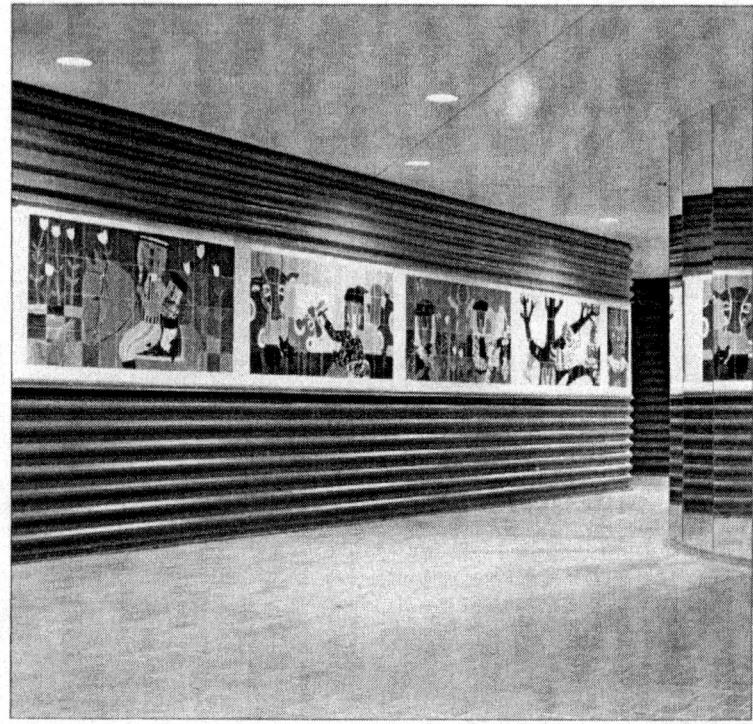

CHILD'S PLAY
Vancouver Children's Hospital

Zbigniew Kupczynski

FINE ART CAN HAVE A MARVELLOUSLY HUMANIZING effect on a public place, especially on a sombre institution like a children's hospital. The new Vancouver Children's Hospital has commissioned numerous lively and light-hearted art works in order to create a friendly and unthreatening atmosphere for its patients. Most of the artists involved have donated their time and talent for very little money.

This month, Gallery features the ceramic tile murals of Zbigniew Kupczynski, a recent addition to the hospital entrance. The murals, which have been hand-painted with low-firing glazes on white tiles, make imaginative, colorful excursions into child's play and fantasy, favorite themes in this artist's paintings and prints. Interstyle Imports of Vancouver, who specialize in custom-designed tiles, provided the materials and did the firing. Kupczynski's work can be seen at the Kupczynski Studio Gallery on Granville Street in Vancouver. ☐

MURAL AT ENTRANCE TO CHILDREN'S HOSPITAL VANCOUVER

Artspeak:
A twice-a-month gallery review
New York, New York
Vol. VI, No. 5,
Nov. 1, 1984

Excerpt from:
The Faces of Zbigniew Kupczynski
By Joseph Merkel

Artists of Central Europe have exploited [Folk Art as inspiration] a great deal, especially after the fine example of Marc Chagall.

Another Folk artist of Polish origin with a powerful voice, Kupczynski can employ this approach to make his personal statement. He takes the same subject matter and the same means but gives each his personal emphasis, thus arriving at a radically different art from Chagall. One could note each different element of Folk Art as seen in this work: color, special motifs, internationally recognized, fantasy, content, style.

Kupczynski is a dynamic and powerful painter and his emotion is expressed basically through his intensity of color. One might say that color is the subject of his paintings, for color is Kupczynski's music.

Biography

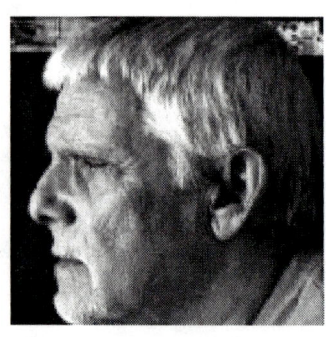

Called "one of the wild boys of Polish art" by Harold Schonberg of the New York Times, Kupczynski was born in Poland and studied at the Academy of Fine Arts and later in Paris. He has exhibited throughout Europe, North America, Australia and Japan, including Musée de la Ville in Paris, Museum of Modern Art in Miami, Carimor Gallery in New York, Museum of Art in Philadelphia (together with Chagall, Picasso, Miro and Klee), Documenta in West Germany and Atagoyama Gallery in Tokyo.

Kupczynski immigrated to Canada in 1971. Today, his work is in private and corporate collections internationally. These include University of Victoria, Children's Hospital in Vancouver, University Hospital in Edmonton, Daon Development, Shell, Esso Resources and Earl's Restaurant chain across Canada. His private collections include Pope John Paul II, Richard Nixon, John Cabot Lodge, Pianist Malcolm Frager, Conductor John Williams and the Bronfman Collection.

In 2001 Kupczynski returned to Poland for two exhibitions, at the Galeria Forma Colour and the Galeria Prezydenta, both in Warsaw. The next year another exhibition of his work was held at the Muzeum Historyczne, also in Warsaw.

Books by and about Kupczynski are *Journey to the Red Desert* (Canadian Marketing Consultants Ltd., 1989), *Three Hundred Years of Kupczynski* (Art West Publishing, 1994) and *Kupczynski* (Jill Pollack, Flower Valley Press, 1996).

He lives in Vancouver with his wife, Eva.